GRAND BORDEAUX CHÂTEAUX

INSIDE THE FINE WINE ESTATES OF FRANCE

Foreword and Tasting Notes **James Suckling**
Text **Philippe Chaix**
Photography **Guillaume de Laubier**

Flammarion

Contents

Remarkable Wines and Cellars

On June 14, 2015, Château Margaux, the famous first-growth wine estate in Bordeaux, hosted a dinner for the international press during the wine fair VinExpo to celebrate its new cellars and wine library designed by renowned British architect Norman Foster. Château Margaux owner Corinne Mentzelopoulos told the crowd of about six hundred people that she had built the structures for "future generations," taking into account the architecture of the past, and she admitted that it had been a daunting experience to try to design and construct a building that would complement the existing structures on the wine estate. Most of the new construction was done underground but the beautiful, natural, and modern style of Foster's winery building forms a modern articulation of the glorious Palladian architecture of the original château that was completed in 1815 by Louis Combes, one of France's greatest architects of the time.

The compelling contemporary architecture and design that have characterized Bordeaux's great wine estates over the last thirty years are a sign of the eminent châteaux's prosperity in France's most famous wine region. This economic success is a direct result of the unprecedented improvement in wine quality, as Bordeaux continues to produce some of the greatest and most prestigious wines in the world.

I began my career as a wine critic in Bordeaux in 1983, during VinExpo. In the early 1980s, the graying facades of the various châteaux showed only traces of past opulence and former success, due to a mostly disastrous decade in the 1970s, with poor wines and a weak economy. Many owners at this time were hoping for a new future for Bordeaux, particularly with an American-consumer wine boom underway.

Yet, at the time, very few wine producers in Bordeaux were aware of the gold aging in their cellars, and that the wines they had in barrel would forever change their world in the Gironde, as well as the world of fine wine in general. The magnificent 1982 vintage was maturing in their cellars, waiting to seduce the wine world, set a new standard for Bordeaux, and define what the wines of the future would be.

I remember my first experience barrel-tasting the 1982 wines. The late Alexis Lichine, then owner of Château Prieuré-Lichine and a legendary wine author, organized a tasting of the sublime vintage from barrel to underline its greatness to a few friends and the press. He was convinced of the quality and he wanted to address an early report in the *New York Times* that had stated the vintage was overrated. Lichine invited many of the best winemakers in the Medoc at the time.

The generosity and the balance of the young reds astounded them all as they tasted from barrel.

Émile Peynaud, the guru enologist of the time, told me a few months later that a great wine was great from the very beginning, no matter if it was in barrel or bottle. The 1982 Bordeaux reds certainly proved this, and the vintage remains a benchmark for modern Bordeaux wines today. The vintage also illustrated the way forward for Bordeaux, by producing more modern and drinkable wines and, in turn, making them more attractive and marketable to the consumer. This coincided with a fundamental change in wine consumption in the United States, with a new group of educated, sophisticated, and affluent people interested in buying the "new modern" Bordeaux—and they bought lots of Bordeaux. Some first growths sold as much as one-quarter of their total production of the 1982 vintage on the US market.

The vintage also set the tone for wine for the next four decades, beginning a fine wine renaissance that had never been seen in the world before. Not only did wine—particularly red wine—become riper and more approachable to drink young, but increasingly excellent quality wines were being produced around the world, from Italy to Australia, and from the United States to Chile. And most of these new wine producers wanted to emulate the quality of great Bordeaux. At the same time, consumers were willing to pay higher prices for fine wines, encouraging producers to make better and better wines. In addition, drinking fine wine, particularly in the United States but more recently in Asia, became fashionable as a symbol of success, good taste, and sophistication.

The affluence of fine Bordeaux wine producers continues today, and a substantial percentage of financial gains is still invested in the infrastructure of estates, for beauty and brand image, as well as to improve the already superb quality of bottled wine. For me, that is the message being conveyed by these new buildings, and it will be the message for future generations.

James Suckling

Right
"The River," as the Gironde is known here, divides the vineyards of the wine estates discussed in the following pages: the estates of Pauillac, Margaux, and Saint-Estèphe stand on the left bank, with those of Pomerol and Saint-Émilion on the right. Here, in Château Montrose, the vines gaze down on the estuary.

Page 8
"With a bottle of Bordeaux, you're buying and drinking architecture," wrote Bernard Pivot in *French Wine: An Illustrated Miscellany*, a statement illustrated by the architectural features from each of the twelve estates in this volume: Angélus, Margaux, Pichon Baron, Cos d'Estournel, Petrus, Cheval Blanc, La Dominique, Montrose, Mouton Rothschild, Lafite Rothschild, Faugères, and Pédesclaux.

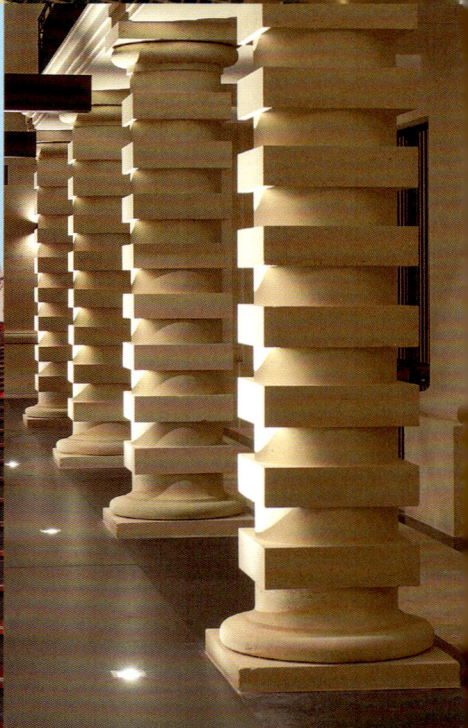

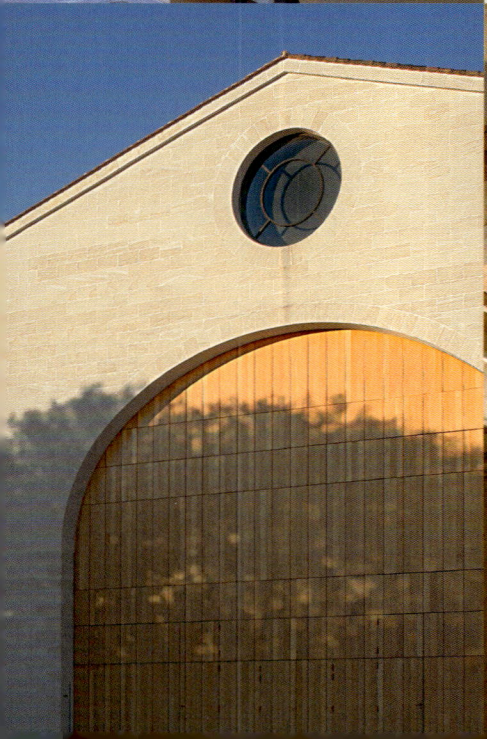

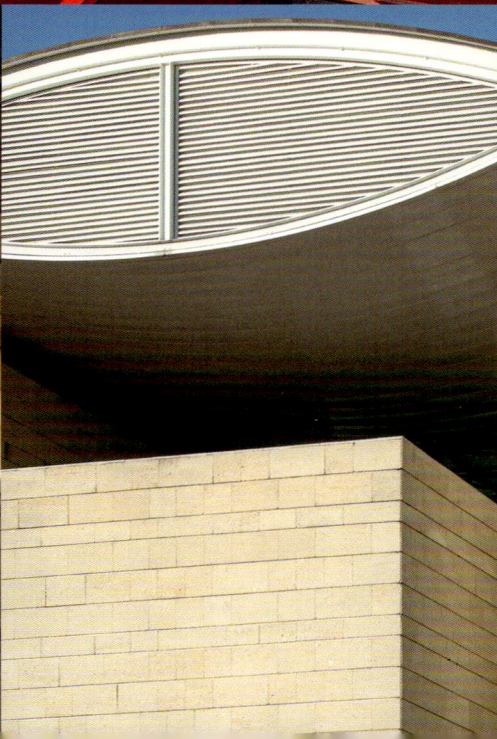

Preface
Why a New Winery?

This is what discovering the Bordelais means: walking through Bordeaux, the city of stone; gazing down at its mirror-like river; feeling the twenty-first-century metropolis as it grows, with its bridges and new buildings; setting off to explore the Médoc and Saint-Émilion, and losing oneself in vineyards striped with paths and lanes; dreaming in those great houses so dear to novelist François Mauriac, and falling in love with the old châteaux (Issan is my favorite); and, finally, lunching in Saint-Émilion itself and savoring one of its great vintages. And the architecture of this micro-region—the world's wine temple—continues to thrive and bewitch. This has been the case for centuries, and the twentieth and twenty-first centuries have certainly contributed their fair share.

Globalization has, if anything, strengthened this remarkable tradition, while the recent phenomenon of wine tourism has brought with it the need for new-look interiors. The present volume invites you on a tour of these wineries: through the aging room, where priceless barrels of successive vintages rest; then the vat house, where the grape harvest—in wood, glass, and steel, and bathed in soft light—is turned into sublime *jus*; and then on to the cellars, in which generations of bottles are laid down, protected behind a layer of precious cork to stop the wine deteriorating.

Wine and architecture suit each other magnificently. And what is the meaning behind the new forms of wine architecture? To provide a worthy backdrop for this "new" love of wine that has developed by leaps and bounds throughout the world—from the Napa Valley to Rioja, by way of Australia, Chile, New Zealand, and South Africa, and not forgetting China. Such buildings arouse sensations and spark strong emotions in all those, of all ages, who are discovering the civilization of wine, glass in hand. These buildings provide the technical equipment essential for the creation of what is now a luxury product: vinification on a plot-by-plot basis calls for a greater number of tanks, while the use of gravity to ensure that the harvest descends without jolting or reversing requires modern wine elevators.

And last but not least, these new wineries display wine as it comes from nature, from the landscape, demonstrating how wine is a natural product—one that emerges from sacred soils and is tended according to the lunar cycle—whose production is increasingly influenced by technology. With vat houses and aging rooms no longer dark and hidden away, the structure of these new wineries is rooted in the environment. Wine requires of architecture that it convey its new globalized message, that it showcase the recent boom in a product that has become, more than ever before in its history, a sign of civilization in all four corners of the world, developing an increasingly aesthetic, sensual, and human relationship to it.

This new chapter in the ageless history of wine is being written by visionary owners, knowledgeable professionals, cellar masters, and vineyard managers, passionate wine lovers, and ingenious architects. Admire them all—and let's enjoy and share our wine with all those we love.

Philippe Chaix

Pauillac

CHÂTEAU LAFITE ROTHSCHILD

BY RICARDO BOFILL

The Inspired Precursor

It was in 1974 that Éric de Rothschild took in hand the destiny of the château—a *premier grand cru classé en 1855* (a first growth classified in 1855)—which has been the property of his family since 1868. "Winegrower by predilection and banker by necessity" would be an apt description of this trailblazer, who invited some of the greatest photographers, including Jacques-Henri Lartigue, Irving Penn, Robert Doisneau, and Richard Avedon, to immortalize the estate, before introducing a touch of contemporary architecture in 1988 with brand new *chais*, or barrel-aging rooms. Éric de Rothschild's approach in building the new *chais*, made necessary by technological developments and a concern for high quality, has been guided by three visions: those of the winemaker, of the engineer, and of the aesthete.

The winemaker requires storehouses that correspond to the increasing complexity of and improving standards in winemaking, especially regarding the harvest and the *cuvaison* (fermentation) plot by plot, which allow the storage of a greater number of barrels in order to ride out the ups and downs of the market. The engineer requires a cellar that is ergonomic and inexpensive to run: studies of the movements of both workers and barrels favor a square or round storehouse in which employees can work more quickly, move around less, and even carry out several tasks at once. Selecting a round form, the aesthete then calls in his friend Ricardo Bofill, acknowledged as a modernist of the greatest stylistic rigor.

There are no ornaments or decoration in the building. The columns are arranged in a sacred circle, illumined by a light well that extends into a dome, the ceilings stretching in a single sweep, the walkway allowing for a variety of viewpoints; all define a space containing concentrically arranged barrels that combine aesthetic impact with practical advantage. To date, several of the world's estates have adopted the circle as the form for the architecture of their cellars, not only in the Bordeaux region but also in China or the US.

Initiates can reach the inner sanctum by taking one of two routes: through deep, dark, intriguing tunnels and cellars, the path of an ancient tradition where each space tells a story, or else by the royal way which runs outside, ordained by Baron Éric and based on the road that led to the entrance of the Tholos Tomb of Clytemnestra near Mycenae—a homage to a civilization in which wine was such an important component.

In this astonishing, specially constructed place, the great wine acquires fresh significance. More than anywhere else, it is perfectly at ease here, reveling in beneficial vibrations during concert evenings and the international string quartet competition that is held every year in this magical venue. Spellbound, concert-goers are aware that the fantastic acoustics of the space vary according to whether the barrels are full or empty. Scented and ethereal, "if Lafite were a painter, it would be Chagall," says Éric de Rothschild, "if it were a composer, it would be Mozart."

Page 13
Upon entering, one is struck
by the serenity of the great
hall, so much so that voices
are lowered to a whisper.
The staircases lead visitors up
to walkways offering a splendid
view of the wine storehouse.

Left
The first aging room to have
been designed by a world-famous
architect, this vast space combines
aesthetic beauty and efficiency
in production. The barrels are
so arranged that they save the
winemakers more than eighteen
hundred miles of walking per
year! The barrels—numbering
from one to two thousand
depending on the year—encircle
an imposing rotunda, a design
which has now become something
of a trend.

Facing page: Octagonal, rather than round, the majesty of the barrel room recalls the Pantheon in Rome, its aesthetic power and extreme practicality compounded by its magical elegance.
Right and below, right: Controlled subdued lighting leads to the *grand chai* underground.
Below: Lafite is the only estate to make every barrel it uses, thus perpetuating the cooper's trade which dates back a thousand years.

Lafite is an authentic château, complete with towers and a terrace bordered by a balustrade. Magnificently exposed and dominating the farm buildings and the vineyard, the château exudes an air of serenity exclusive to buildings with a venerable history. The estate occupies the prettiest hillocks of Pauillac. As Éric de Rothschild wrote, "Lafite is harmony between nature and man."

"I do love Lafite. I love the precision: the intuitive and scientific knowledge of vine-tending and winemaking, which is as nothing without the skill of man."
Éric de Rothschild

CHÂTEAU LAFITE ROTHSCHILD 2010

Believe the hype. Lafite is perfect in 2010. The nose is amazing, with sweet tobacco, dark chocolate, and currants. The taste is full and powerful with amazing minerals, currants, and bitter chocolate. It starts off slowly and then finishes with a bang. This is really layered and wonderful: it's like gazing into the blue sky in wonder after tasting this young wine. It just goes on and on. Stunning.

James Suckling

Left: More modern cement tanks, in which the various plots are vinified with the utmost care.
Below, left: A traditional *cuvier* with its oak vats.
Below: The estate's *tonnellerie* or barrel-making facility: five coopers work here all year round.
Facing page: The entrance designed by the architect for the underground storehouse beneath the vines is positively regal. The wine is vinified in the vat room before aging in the *chai*.

Margaux

CHÂTEAU MARGAUX

BY NORMAN FOSTER

1815–2015
Two Centuries of Architecture

Something had to be done! First, it was necessary to get to grips with the new technical demands resulting from decades of evolution in winemaking methods, which had brought ever-greater precision and quality (thirty tanks were produced thirty years ago; the figure is one hundred today). A special vat was needed for the vinification of the Pavillon Blanc, a white wine produced in Margaux since the seventeenth century from a single grape variety—Sauvignon—which had recently attained true excellence. Separate buildings dedicated to research and development were needed to improve results. Collections of past vintages were to be stored in a hugely ambitious *vinothèque*. And, finally, as wine tourism continued to boom, a room worthy of the most famous and majestic château in the whole of the Médoc had to be furbished to accommodate visitors from all over the world (more than ten thousand a year), with the aim of helping them discover and understand the wine.

Corinne Mentzelopoulos handed the weighty but enthralling task of designing and executing this project to Norman Foster. Thus, across two centuries, from 1815 to 2015, the utopian revolutionary Louis Combes—the great Bordeaux architect who designed the city hall and the Grand Hôtel, and who knew how to embellish a Bordeaux château like no one else—extends a hand to his twenty-first-century colleague whose approach is no less pure and luminous. After prolonged study and plentiful exchanges, Paul Pontallier, general manager of the estate, and Lord Foster defined a coherent architectural brief for the future, one that would renovate the stone village without superfluous additions, while paying tribute to history and permanence with precision and humility.

The enthusiast—for one does not happen upon this hallowed temple of enological civilization by chance or pop in while passing by—is now led into a vast showroom, a onetime agricultural building with a towering wooden roof-frame, where the history of the property from 1619 to the present day is displayed in a modern yet understated way.

Passing in front of the château, which appears to be lifted skyward by its magnificent approach of plane trees, the twenty-two steps of its precinct, and its Ionic columns, visitors already stand at the beginning of the "Foster itinerary." A seamless extension of the farm buildings, the new Pavillon Blanc vat room is topped by a roof-tile hat borne on metal umbrella-shaped supports painted white to impart lightness. Reached down a spiral stairway, the tanks are located beneath a metal "Médoc" floor. Through a continuous and subtly articulated space, visitors make their way along the R&D buildings to emerge in the aging houses for the first and second years, which were erected in previous decades and have been preserved intact, and which display the same qualities of grandeur and forward-thinking as Monsieur Mentzelopoulos when he took over and overhauled the property in 1977. Strolling by the cooperage, where the barrels are made out of oak from central France, visitors recall that attaining such heights of perfection requires craftsmen who are masters of time-honored techniques.

Finally, their steps lead them to Lord Foster's *vinothèque*: a great, long wine library built of raw concrete over four levels, the upper ones being accessed along a suspended promenade. Here, time stands still, and from the tasting room the eye gets lost gazing down the endless nave.

Consummate professionals like Lord Foster and Paul Pontallier have magically transformed this mythical domain, handing down to future generations a modernized location, at once unobstructed and efficient. A fine legacy indeed. Happy birthday, Château Margaux!

Page 27
The château built by Louis
Combes in 1810 can be glimpsed
through the metal "branches"
supporting the roof of the
new wine storehouse, designed
by Norman Foster, which
opened in June 2015.

Left
Foster's building glides
unobtrusively, in perfect
continuity with the old *chais*.
The peristyle of the nineteenth-
century château can be seen in
the background. According
to the architect, he wanted to
leave precedence to the château,
and therefore chose to build
the new *chai* under a large
traditional roof concealing
an open and versatile space.

It was a daring move to ask the architect who built the viaduct at Millau, among other major constructions, to intervene on a listed historic domain. Though intended to be in perfect harmony with the nineteenth-century château, the interior of the winery had to be resolutely contemporary. Mission accomplished: here, steel reigns supreme.
Facing page: Partitions to the vat room.
Right: A spiral staircase leads to the tanks in the mezzanine and to a tasting room.
Below and below, right: Opening onto nature, the storehouse is illuminated by a series of light wells.

Sculpture-like, the twelve white-painted steel "trees" that support the roof of the new aging facility remind the architect of the bare branches of the plane trees in winter. Simplicity itself in appearance, its structure offers a reinterpretation of the region's traditional roofs. The result of prolonged research, the glass and steel partitions afford a design of great flexibility. The architect thus fulfills both the technical specifications and the aesthetic demands of the château.

"The genius of the place consists in producing wines of inimitable aromatic finesse and complexity, of admirable density to the palate, and yet which remain astonishingly soft."
Paul Pontallier

CHÂTEAU MARGAUX 2009

This possesses a special nose of blackberries and roses—lots of them. Full and powerful on the palate, with big chewy tannins that are polished and in perfect proportion. This is a monumental wine that is built for aging. Analytically, it is the most concentrated Margaux ever—even better than when I tasted it in spring.

James Suckling

The tasting room reserved for professionals looks onto the vines, with the terrace providing views over the château. Unlike the *chais* of the past, here all is open onto nature, to resonate harmoniously with the landscape. These new installations provide the château with tools worthy of its reputation and of the quality of its wine.

Facing page, right, and below, right:
Built in prestressed concrete, the *vinothèque*
leads through to the tasting room for visitors,
which has a table also designed by Norman
Foster. At the end of the visit, guests move
from the vat room flooded with daylight to the
shade of the spectacular wine library. Three
hundred feet long, the building can contain three
thousand five hundred bottles of the finest years
from 1848 in optimum storage conditions.
Below: The second-year storehouse is connected
to the new *vinothèque*, which was constructed
beneath a plot of vines in order to leave the
landscape unaltered.

Margaux is the only classified growth to bear the name of its appellation. A rare example of French neo-Palladian style erected in the nineteenth century, the château has been called the Versailles of the Médoc. The most majestic in the entire region, its dazzling Ionic peristyle can be seen at the end of the avenue of hundred-year-old plane trees. The spirit of the place is bewitching, unique.

Pauillac

CHÂTEAU MOUTON ROTHSCHILD

BY BERNARD MAZIÈRES
& RICHARD PEDUZZI

Wine on Center Stage

Forging bonds between wine and the visual arts and defending innovative architecture has become a "Mouton" tradition. When Baron Philippe de Rothschild took charge of the estate in 1922, he introduced two original initiatives. First, he took the historic decision to bottle the production at the château, thereby cutting out the middlemen. To this end, he built a cellar on a single floor, without posts or any other obstacles, that can store up to one thousand barrels in ideal conditions. This architectural tour de force—a great success—was designed for him by Charles Siclis, a friend to whom he had offered his patronage, and the architect of two playhouses in Pigalle, Paris: the Théâtre Saint-Georges and the Théâtre des Mathurins.

The spectacular alignment of the barrels, the subdued yet theatrical lighting in the vast astylar hall with its elongated volumes, and even the statue of Bacchus who looks out at visitors and seems to conduct them through this miraculous space have led several other estates to imitate the design of this *chai*.

In the estate's museum today, visitors can also engross themselves in a pocket history of modern art in the form of wine labels that have appeared once a year since 1950, signed by a diverse range of artists such as Jean Cocteau, Léonor Fini, Miró, Dalí, Chagall, Balthus, Picasso, Baselitz, and Keith Haring.

When Philippine de Rothschild took over the reins in 2005, she quickly realized the necessity for new building extensions. Shortly after, one afternoon, Richard Peduzzi's cell phone rang. Let him take up the story:

"One day in 2007, I was away in Italy. Strolling along some wild stony path, I got a call from Philippine de Rothschild. She said, 'So, now I know what I want you to do at Mouton.' She went on to outline the structural works and the wholesale transformation she'd planned for the château, in particular the conception of a new wine storehouse. 'I remembered your sets, the way you treat volume and proportion. And I recalled the links we both had with the theater.' Arriving in Mouton one day, I saw an enormous boat crossing the Gironde and it seemed to sail amid the vines, as if lost. I thought back to the prow of the boat I'd designed for a set for *Tristan und Isolde* that plunges into the marsh fog."

With these few words, the great set designer, who has worked with some of the most fascinating directors of the past thirty years (Patrice Chéreau and Luc Bondy, to name but two), alludes to the vast nave of glass and wood, which is both a stage on which the great play—or, as it used to be called, "mystery"—of wine is performed and a place of work with airy spaces and clearly laid-out passages that is a pleasure for its personnel to work in.

Forming an effective team with the architect Bernard Mazières, a recognized specialist in wine and vine architecture, Richard Peduzzi here bequeaths to Bordeaux and Mouton a significant project defined by the harmonious disposition of its spaces and volumes, the subtle arrangement of its perspectives, and the serene symmetry of the two imposing pediments framing the château; although handled with contemporary aplomb, together they conjure up the great age of French provincial ecclesiastical architecture.

Page 45
The pediment of the
new vat room echoes that
of the previous aging facility
seen here on the right.
At harvest, grapes are
brought in through the
doors on the upper level.

Right
The vines seem to greet
the huge stone building,
gleaming in the sun, and
housing both the old
storehouse and the Musée
du Vin dans l'Art. Visitors
come here in droves to
see extremely rare pieces
of silverwork, ivory, and
porcelain that bear witness
to the age-old dialogue
between art and wine.

Like a great theater of wine, the new aging facility comes complete with stage, set, and lighting.

Facing page: A striking perspective down the upper floor where the grapes are brought in, structured by an imposing oak roof-frame.

Right and below: High- and low-angle views of the vat house built in a harmonious blend of wood and steel, providing ample views of the work going on below.

Below, right: Close-up of a vat in which two of the wooden staves have been replaced by panels of glass, allowing the curious visitor to observe the wine within.

Left
True to the estate's artistic
principles, the tasting
table held up by two sheep
(*moutons*) is a veritable
sculpture that stands for the
Mouton spirit of hospitality.

Page 53
Every year the labels on
bottles of Mouton Rothschild
wrap the wine in art:
2010 saw the reproduction
of an illustration by the
American artist Jeff Koons,
inspired by a fresco in Pompeii
representing Venus emerging
from the waves.

"The soul of Mouton? I would define it as rooted in two entities: a classic fine wine grown on an exceptional terroir and a place of art and beauty."
Philippine de Rothschild

CHÂTEAU MOUTON ROTHSCHILD 2010

This is pure Mouton. The aromas in this wine are so fabulous, it immediately brought to mind the 1947, one of the great classics of Mouton. Menthol, mint, subtle eucalyptus, currants, and dark fruits on the nose. Full-bodied, with super intense and powerful fruit and tannins. So unique for a first growth. Almost all Cabernet (94% Cabernet Sauvignon and 6% Merlot). Magnificent. This is clearly better than 2009.

James Suckling

Soil, history, art, and wine form the magic square that endows Mouton with its incomparable personality. The historic Musée du Vin dans l'Art boasts an exhibition room devoted uniquely to art and to wine labels. Its creator, Philippine de Rothschild, appears in the reflection of this photograph by Karl Lagerfeld.

CHÂTEAU PICHON BARON

BY JEAN DE GASTINES
PATRICK DILLON & ALAIN TRIAUD

Renaissance(s)

In the years 1980–85, the Pompidou Centre in Paris actively sought to promote and encourage new architectural talent through major exhibitions and research workshops. Candidates were invited to exercise their creativity by revisiting the architecture of winemaking estates—in particular the Domaine de Pichon-Longueville, recently acquired by the Group AXA, which had lost its way a little. The prizewinners were architects Jean de Gastines and Patrick Dillon, with AXA's founding president, Claude Bébéar, as chair of the jury. The property's old cellars were completely demolished, leaving the architectural page blank and ready for a bold design that would fulfill the most exacting specifications, both for the production areas and the visitor spaces.

The prizewinning project can still be visited and appreciated today, since it remains exactly as it was in 1988. It complements rather than contrasts with the two main features of its surroundings: the Renaissance manor and the scenery of the Médoc. With its old, somewhat busy décor and its many stylistic references, the entirely restored château remains intact. Instead of upstaging it, the new plans sought to enhance it, treating it like an elegant ancestor who is to be respected and affectionately greeted. Half-buried in front of the château, the aging room is an entirely horizontal structure, with a pond in the center that accentuates the mirror effects. In a grand theatrical gesture, the long wall along the roadside has been preserved and enlarged to form a backdrop for the storehouse. The Médoc landscape provided the two prizewinners with the elements that would form their architectural idiom. Winegrowing areas are generally extremely linear, with low stone walls and seemingly endless rows of vines scored with pathways and lanes, while each estate tries to hide its not-so-well-kept secret behind a lofty and sturdy enclosure. The Médoc is a perfect example. Indeed, it was this very scenery, into which Pichon-Longueville neatly fits along the edge of the wine road, that was the inspiration for the gloriously simplified geometrical forms—squares, circles, and small obelisks—that punctuate the horizontal and vertical lines of stone. Romanesque art is omnipresent and is joined by the arcane symbolism of the Enlightenment, which was inscribed on the facade by the master masons who worked here and was carried further afield by others of a speculative cast of mind. Beneath the long, horizontal structure, visitors discover ingeniously arranged cellars, storage areas, and the circular vat surrounded by inward-leaning columns. In the work rooms, underground stylized Romanesque capitals offer confirmation of the clarity and decorative unity of the whole structure.

In 2006, a new cellar was built by the architect Alain Triaud: a vault formed of a prestressed concrete shell, all understated elegance and exemplary proportions. Here, the precious barrels of Château Pichon-Longueville repose in a sober haven, and the château attracts visitors from all over the world.

Page 59 and left
These two views of the
entrance building to the new
winery provide a perfect
illustration of the stylistic
investigations undertaken by
the two architects: the results
are visible throughout the
estate. Delivered in 1988,
the new installations are the
second contemporary creation
in the Médoc, after Lafite.
The idea of placing such
a novel construction in the
landscape, half-burying it
to keep the views over the old
château intact and having
it reflected in water, was,
however, resolutely innovative.
The remit for the château
itself was to provide it with
a plinth and so enhance its
prestige. Horizontal in form,
this architecture recalls the
monuments of Ancient Egypt
with its funerary mastabas.
The new constructions conceal
the work and circulation
areas: after offering a welcome
to visitors—a new concept
in 1988—they conduct them
underground.

Left and facing page: A new underground barrel-aging facility, designed and built by Alain Triaud in 2006, now joins the one erected in 1988. The idea is to optimize ease of movement for those working in the space, which means no pillars, no load-bearing walls, and the use of prestressed concrete in the great French tradition that includes engineer Nicolas Esquillan and master architect Auguste Perret.
Below, left: The large disk of light that opens at the summit of the dome is brightly reflected in the mirror-like pool in front of the buildings opposite the entrance to the château.
Below: The hall is laid out like a temple, through which visitors can stroll beneath closely spaced columns that accentuate the almost religious atmosphere.

The new vat room signals
the triumph of technology
deployed in the service
of winemaking of the highest
quality. With stainless steel
for the tanks and the spiral
staircase, the hall resembles
an engine room monitored by
a control panel, thus bringing
modernity to the world of
Pichon. The aging facility is
arranged lengthwise, while the
hall containing the vats is laid
out in a circle. Benefiting from
overhead lighting, the hall
is raised by inclined columns
topped by Romanesque-style
capitals that hark back to the
venerable history of wine.

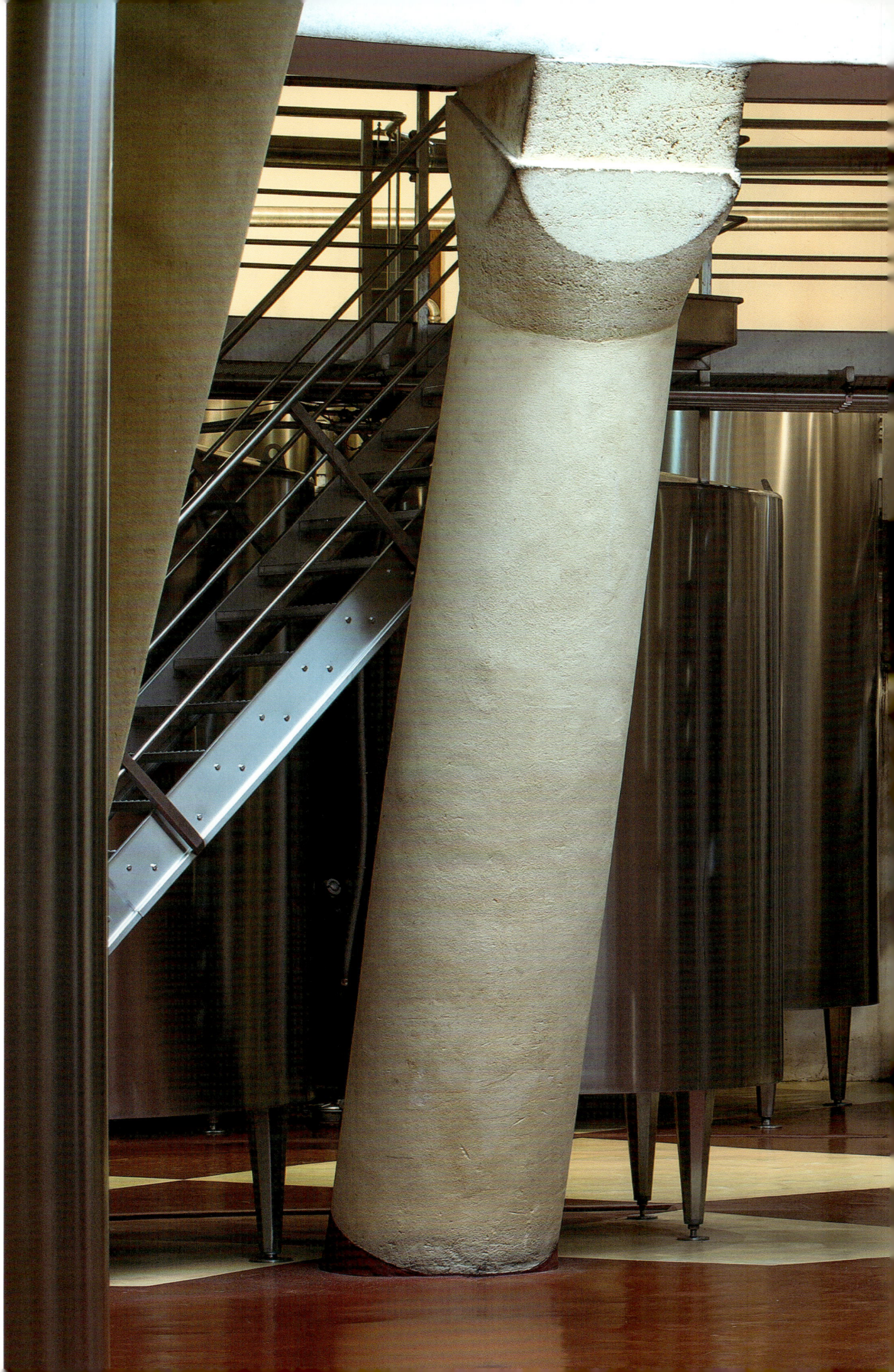

"The grandeur of a great growth comes from the soil. Our duty is to let it express itself fully."
Christian Seely

CHÂTEAU PICHON-LONGUEVILLE BARON 2009

Amazing aromas of ripe currants and plums with flowers.
Full-bodied, with super-fine tannins and wonderful fruit. It is energized.
Reminds me of the 1990 vintage, which is a legend. Try after 2020.

James Suckling

Left: In the estate shop, visitors are introduced to the entire range of Bordeaux bottles—a family as famous as the wine itself and which now forms part of the French legend that devotees from every continent come to meet: Magnum, Jeroboam, Methuselah, Salmanazar, Nebuchadnezzar, Solomon, Sovereign, and Primat.

Below, left: A cozy and comfortable setting adapted to wine-tasting is ensured by the use of warm woods and by subtle lighting arrangements.

Below: The passageway to the barrel-aging room. A side-effect of globalization, wine tourism has persuaded many châteaux to open their doors to the thousands of lovers of fine wines from around the world who wish to visit these legendary centers of production.

Facing page: In 1850 Baron Raoul de Longueville inherited part of the property founded by his ancestors: this was to become the Domaine de Pichon-Longueville, the name changing to Pichon Baron in 2012. Proud of his heritage and ambitious on his own account, in 1851 the baron built a romantic estate in a Renaissance idiom. This style—a frequent choice during an era rediscovering historical architecture—is instantly recognizable by the two pointed towers resembling witches' hats that today peer down into the mirror-like basin installed for the purpose. At present, this edifice houses visitors' rooms and reception halls.

Saint-Estèphe

CHÂTEAU MONTROSE

BY BERNARD MAZIÈRES
& JACQUES GARCIA

The Spirit of the Eighteenth Century

Legend has it that the château is called Montrose due to its immediately recognizable hillocks which are covered in rose-pink heather that served as a landmark for sailors on the Garonne river. When, in 2006, Martin and Olivier Bouygues became the owners of the château—whose wine is classified as a *deuxième grand cru*, a second growth—they embarked on an ambitious program of works. Taking place over five long years from 2007–13, these works ensured the continuing and trouble-free management and production of the estate's three exemplary wines.

Eighteenth-century architecture, the predominant style in the Bordeaux region and in the city itself, is the reference at Montrose thanks to the domain's first great reformer, Mathieu Dollfus: an industrialist from Alsace, who built the "Village of Montrose" with its alleys, little squares, and streets lined with winegrowers' houses and tiny workshops, all restored to their former glory today. This exceptional renovation program was directed with a firm and resolute hand by Mélissa Bouygues, president of the winery, assisted by managing director Hervé Berland, and under the architectural direction of Bernard Mazières. Its central element and Montrose's veritable hallmark is the *Grand Chai*—the storehouse in which the estate's first wine is matured and the linchpin of the entire project. This cellar (10,700 square feet, with 36-foot ceilings), where the humidity and temperature are monitored with extreme precision, housed its first vintage, Château Montrose 2013, in 2014.

Majestic in its lines, this buried storehouse, which is invisible from the outside, is a work of masterly understatement, like a chapter house in which silence and respect reign. The summit of the gallery walkway affords dramatic perspectives and views of the perfect details of the finish and the refined floor pattern. Entering via the courtyard, visitors are struck by what is a simultaneous tribute to the French grand style of the eighteenth-century Enlightenment, to the cult of the great wines laid down in their stone monastery, and to an architectural simplicity that makes one forget what a technical tour de force it really is. The monastic idiom is further underscored by the subdued lighting in the first-level vaulting.

Becoming famous overnight, the new cellar at Montrose is a truly extraordinary monument: it is, in Paul Valéry's words, "a building that speaks."

Page 73
As if on the threshold to some enchanted kingdom, the closed gate is thrown open to reveal a magnificent perspective.

Right
In June 2015, this marvelous room was chosen by the Commanderie de Bontemps as the prestigious venue for their no less prestigious Fête de la Fleur celebrating the flowering of the vine. Magnificently restored, the lighting alone amounts to an architectural tour de force. The red-banded wooden barrels on the black granite floor glint in the light.

Facing page: Located at the northernmost point of the vineyard and facing the ocean, the estate of Montrose stands opposite the Gironde estuary. This vast stretch of water acts as natural climate control, while the sloping terrain offers the vineyard drainage without artificial aids.
Right: The French flag flutters above the wind turbine that used to bring up water to irrigate the vines.
Below: A gate opens out onto the fields.
Below, right: The vintagers: whole teams of these heroes of the harvest have remained faithful to the property for several generations.

Page 78
Vitis vinifera: a leaf from this wild creeper has here been "trained" into a bracket light.

Page 79
The modern rhythm of the carved columns in the great barrel-aging room would not look out of place in a construction by eighteenth-century architect Claude Nicolas Ledoux; and indeed, the portico was inspired by his Royal Saltworks at Arc-et-Senans, in the Franche-Comté in eastern France.

Left
Visitors are greeted by blooms of cosmos—pink, of course. Perched on a small promontory, the unpretentious property is sufficiently elevated to serve as a landmark for boats sailing down the estuary.

"I fell for the charm of the place.
A broad, continuous stretch of land facing
the river—it is an absolutely unique site."
Martin Bouygues

CHÂTEAU MONTROSE 2009

Blueberries, currants, and Indian spices on the nose follow through
to a full body, with ultra-fine tannins and a lovely finish. Intense
and refined; it's a real beauty that goes on for minutes. It leaves you
speechless. Better and cleaner than the great 1990. Try in 2022.

James Suckling

SECOND GRAND CRU CLASSÉ EN 1855

Château Montrose

2009

Saint-Estèphe

Left: Admirable craftsmanship on the balustrade above the barrel-aging facility.
Below: A monumental fireplace stands among extremely sober volumes, while the chandeliers recall hoops ringing the casks.
Facing page: The décor in the traditional and welcoming tasting room was orchestrated by Mélissa Bouygues, president of Montrose.

Saint-Estèphe

CHÂTEAU COS D'ESTOURNEL

BY JEAN-MICHEL WILMOTTE

"Let yourself go a little, Monsieur Wilmotte."

Once upon a time there was a dandified marquis from Bordeaux who had eyes only for the Indies, his horses, and his wine. Louis-Gaspard d'Estournel, known as the "Maharajah of Saint-Estèphe," was born in the reign of Louis XV (1762) and died, penniless, during that of Napoléon III (1853). From the Indies the marquis brought back a taste for the exotic that Stendhal—a great writer who once visited the estate for a day—described as a "just-back-from-the-Indies" kind of ambiance, with wooden carvings from Zanzibar, palm trees aligned like a guard of stock-still Sikhs, sculptures of lotuses scattered here and there, pretty unicorns, and triumphal arches surmounted by lions. Almost two centuries later, these strange and delightful buildings, devoted solely to the making of a wine—Chateau Cos d'Estournel, a second growth sought after all over the world—still stand there before us, like a daydream inspired by the *Arabian Nights*.

In 2008, just a few years after acquiring the winery, Michel Reybier decided to have its aging rooms restored and extended. The visitor reception areas were entrusted to Jacques Garcia, while Jean-Michel Wilmotte set to work on the core of the reactor—a vast new cellar of 51,600 square feet over two levels—aided by the Bordeaux agency BPM and collaborating with the chief architect for French historic buildings, Alain-Charles Perrot. The reception halls, too, whisk us off to an imagined Orient. Once through the monumental door—the very same through which the precious harvest was carried once a year—elephants guide us to the gates of Paradise: the *vinothèque*, with its fabulous, venerable bottles of *grand cru* jealously guarded by their fellows. From there one enters the rebuilt barrel-aging room. Backing on to the old pagoda, the *chais* and vats have been reconfigured to fit into the historical farm buildings, while new foundations have been dug, fifty-five feet deep in some places. From the outside, however, visitors see little more than a sturdy stone wall and might never guess the magical kingdom that lies behind it.

The new cellar is accessed over footbridges built of backlit glass blocks through which one can admire the wooden, glass, and steel frame supported by stays—the only three materials used in the construction. Metal is taken up in the wine tanks, wood echoes the barrels, while glass creates an appearance of lightness. Pipes conveying wine run in all directions. This is the upper floor—the "Médoc" floor—because here gravity is used in the winemaking process, to preserve the complex flavor and freshness of the grape. There are no pumps: just barrel and wine-tank elevators—and seventy-two tronconic tanks of various sizes, which hold a harvest picked on a plot-by-plot basis and left to settle prior to the mysterious process of *assemblage*, or blending. The barrels below are naturally spotlit by the daylight entering through columns of glass and stainless steel, while the dense color of the materials confers an elegant and enigmatic air on the scene. "Hi-tech alchemy" is perhaps the best description of this operational yet beautiful place.

Leaving this atmosphere of timeless purity, visitors once again encounter elephants—topiary shrubs that lead them to the tasting room; here, the great beasts conclude their walk in the form of sconces on the long white walls, gazing down at the tasters as they savor and get closer to the heart of the peerless wine for which this audacious venue was imagined. So, Monsieur Wilmotte did indeed "let himself go"—spectacularly—just as the master of the house, Michel Reybier, requested.

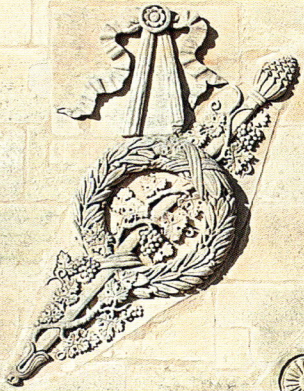

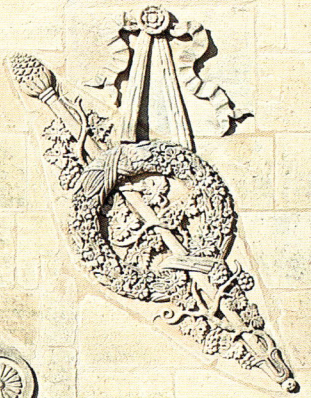

Page 89: A door from the Sultanate of Zanzibar, through which the grape harvest used to enter before being taken to the vat house. One can easily imagine the delight of Louis-Gaspard d'Estournel, "the maharajah of Saint-Estèphe," as he looked at this door, which declared both his love of the Orient, as well as the universal appeal of the great vintages of Bordeaux being set up in the Médoc.
Left: The oldest bottles on the property (1865 is the most venerable vintage) repose in the cozy, calm, almost clandestine wine library.
Below, left and facing page: Opening through to the dazzling glass vat room, the huge blue doors offer a striking contrast.
Below: The atmosphere and subdued lighting of the vast reception halls were designed by Jacques Garcia as a tribute to Louis-Gaspard d'Estournel and his fondness for all things Oriental.

Everything conspires to astound, impress, and beguile visitors in the winemaking hall. Built in metal, stainless steel, and glass, its design combines admirable purity with immense power, like something from a science-fiction film. Flowing and interlocking, each object fulfills a precise role. Vinified in seventy-two tanks, grapes from individual plots are kept separate. A height difference of several yards between the platform where the grapes are brought in during harvest and the vat means they can be transferred via gravity rather than pumps. Standing beneath this spectacular wooden ceiling, the viewer is struck by a feeling of light, which, reflecting off other surfaces, makes for a unique space.

Left and below: The equipment in this gleaming temple is perfectly adapted to the men working here. Looking tiny, they glide over the footbridges, silent guardians of the fermenting grapes.
Facing page: The barrel-aging room resembles an underground glass basilica. The glass and steel posts are a real work of art, standing out like jewels against the black-painted walls and ceiling.
Page 96: The elegant Manueline tower, the oldest vestige of the estate, looks down on the Gironde from a height of more than ninety feet.
Page 97: With the Bordeaux road skirting around it, the domain stands on a slightly elevated plot of land. Borne away to the past, visitors gaze on the three curious-looking turrets, resembling tiny castles from the *Arabian Nights*—the stuff of dreams.

"Year after year, whatever the conditions, Cos d'Estournel owes it to itself to produce a wine commensurate with its reputation and which fulfills the expectations of all those who love our château."
Aymeric de Gironde

CHÂTEAU COS D'ESTOURNEL 2009

Classic Cos with so much spice and fruit, yet refined and sexy. Powerful with super silky tannins. Full-bodied, yet incredibly compacted. This is so tight and rich, with layers of fruit and tannins and a finish that last for minutes on the palate. I asked the head of Cos, Jean-Guillaume Prats, what the alcohol on the wine was, and he said 14.8% alcohol and 3.58 pH. Fabulous. Try after 2021.

James Suckling

Below and facing page: As visitors proceed to the tasting room—whose technical specifications ensure the perfect conditions for the delicate exercise of exploring the bouquet and savor of the wine—they are accompanied everywhere by elephants, mighty symbols of wisdom.
Left and below, left: As ornaments and topiary hedges, the animals keep vigil. As one walks past the refectory for the vintagers, one thinks of those unsung heroes whose second home this will be during the festival of the grape harvest.

CHÂTEAU PÉDESCLAUX

BY JEAN-MICHEL WILMOTTE

The Architecture of Transparency

It had once been a charterhouse, but its delightful volumes and delicate ornaments had greatly suffered over the years, and it was on the brink of falling down. Two years ago, the new owners, Françoise and Jacky Lorenzetti, entrusted Jean-Michel Wilmotte with the project of resurrecting the château and building a new wine storehouse: it is a work that has become a veritable manifesto of the architect's art and creativity.

The starting point was a large piece of land, a small property, an ample courtyard, various hangars, and a slight slope opening out onto the landscape. The finished result is an elegant château, in stone and glass, with, just next to it, the revolutionary new *chai*—a unified and efficient building that has brought production back into the heart of the estate. Set on esplanades of spotless white concrete drenched in sunlight, it is reminiscent of those Greek or Roman temples on whose peristyles vestals celebrated pagan cults.

Thanks to two fully glazed extensions either side, shimmering with silver, the château has returned to center stage. In the tasting room to the right of the entrance, visitors enjoy south-facing vistas over the most scenic part of the estate and over the estuary of the Garonne, on which they may glimpse rows of *carrelets*—fishing cabins recalling a bygone age.

The vat hall is entirely glazed, allowing the wine's development to be observed from the outside, and is enveloped by a frontage in bronze anodized aluminum blades that move with the sun. Such transparency—so beloved to Jacky Lorenzetti—is a deliberate statement, a bold signature that opposes the underground cellars and buried storerooms of yesteryear. Transparency also implies togetherness and conviviality, values dear to this rugby enthusiast—a communal sport if ever there was one. And, last but not least, this notion of transparency is carried through to the vats' position beside a canopy of vines: after taking in the vinestocks less than twenty feet away, the eye is soon drawn to the interior.

The building rests on and is supported by sixty standing tanks. Here, structure is dictated by the process of gravity winemaking. From harvest to bottling, the precious bunches of grapes are cocooned, never manhandled, and are treated plot by plot prior to blending.

To optimize temperature control, the barrel-aging room, with its barrels beneath the vat facility, lies half underground. Built out of the noblest materials, both raw and natural—such as black quartz concrete and wood—this "cathedral" also boasts a monumental staircase, an initiatory work resembling a medieval masterpiece by Jean-Michel Wilmotte, whose vision here recalls monks going about their work in silence.

In this welcoming atmosphere there rests a sea of barrels hooped in black. Served by a host of twenty-first-century technicians in an open, light-filled universe of aluminum and metal, the sacred wine is laid in total communion with nature.

Arranged in sequences, the landscaping is simplicity itself, offering visitors a variety of vistas—different outlooks that bring out the beauty of this tiny corner of the world, and enhanced by what is a respectful yet audacious construction placed entirely in the service of a great wine whose resurrection is well underway.

Page 105
The ambitious new vat house
makes a grand statement
of architectural modernity.
Its glass frontage reflects the
enlarged, former charterhouse,
creating total harmony
between past and present.

Right
The steel floor of the mezzanine
on the first level is a hymn
to modern technology. A pair
of tank-elevators brings up
the *jus* and transfers it to
fixed tanks by way of gravity
rather than with pumps.
In this way, the wine is treated
as gently as possible.

Architectural features illustrating the extremely high quality of the technical elements and the exterior.

Facing page: A view of the light playing on two upright tanks.

Right: From the garden planted with box and holm cork oaks, the new winery tapers into the sky.

Below: The stainless-steel door to a tank. The number corresponds to the plot number of the grapes inside.

Below, right: Seen from the white terrace, the rows of tanks look like columns supporting the building.

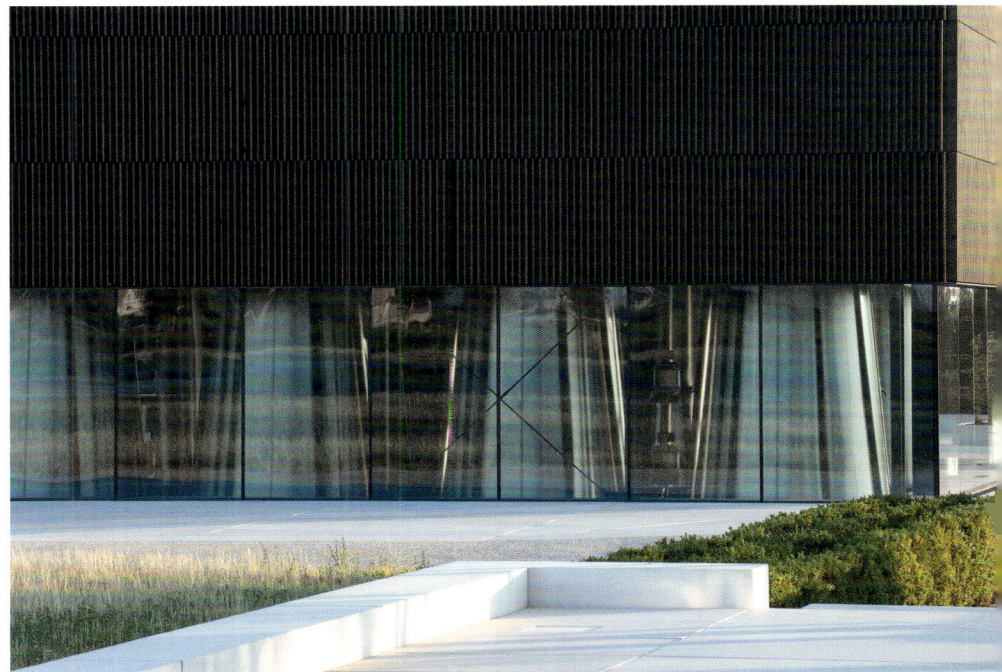

Hugging the earth and far from the hustle and bustle of the harvest, the visits, and the tastings, the barrel-aging room in the basement offers striking perspectives. Its blond-colored wooden barrels borne on concrete piers shimmer in the soft, warm light. Today, it is the 2013 and 2014 vintages that repose here, watched over by a ballet of silent shadows, the estate's most devoted collaborators.

Taransaud
FRANCE

Ref. 116 M+

PxB
PAUILLAC
2014

"(Our aim?) To make an authentic architectural statement, to modernize without severing our roots, to perpetuate tradition, to respect the terroir of Pauillac and preserve its grapes by using gentle gravity-flow methods, and to strive continually for perfection."
Françoise Lorenzetti

CHÂTEAU PÉDESCLAUX 2014

Amazing quality.... Their best wine ever. Superb balance of fruit and ripe tannins with a velvety texture, yet tightly grained and luscious. And what length! It lasts for minutes on the palate.

James Suckling

At once buoyant and luminous, the precious vines at the foot of the charterhouse and its extensions perform an eloquent duet. "Take the two glass boxes around the château: they give it wings," architect Jean-Michel Wilmotte observes. On the floor above, guests are accommodated in romantically decorated rooms. The balcony in the central room presents a splendid view over the Garonne.

Left: A little "dovecote" lands in the tasting room.
Below, left: The reception hall with its wall of bottles.
Below: The brilliantly designed spiral stairway that acts as a counterpoint to the dovecote.
Facing page: Lit by two imposing chandeliers created by Murano master glassmaker Aristide Najean, the tasting room is furnished with a table whose gloriously glossy surface is made of stone and steel dust.

Sited in the area occupied by the wet docks, the Cité du Vin rises like a sculpture on the riverbank. Since its opening in spring 2016, boats leaving from the center of Bordeaux take visitors on a slow journey to Pauillac or Libourne during which they can enjoy views of the great estates on both sides of the Gironde river.

LA CITÉ

DU VIN

A Wine Glass on the Garonne River

A site specifically intended to help visitors discover, appreciate, and understand the civilization of wine, situated in one of the cities in which it has been elevated to its highest peak, resembles a wine glass placed on the Garonne river. In 2011, the city of Bordeaux decided to endow itself with a major center for culture and tourism of international status, which in turn called for an iconic building: a strong, immediately identifiable statement combining present-day concerns and respect for the remarkable character of its location—the wet docks of Bordeaux, dominated by the majestic Chaban-Delmas Bridge—which would embody power, prosperity, and dynamism.

This new facility foregrounds the universality of wine, with its many cultural facets and modernity: mythological wine; wine as sculptor of the landscape; wine that binds winegrowing communities together; wine that prompted exploration on the high seas; wine as communion between men, as ritual, as social symbol; and finally, the wine we drink, the wine that has so long inspired artists and poets.

The response of the XTU agency, headed by Nicolas Desmazière and Anouk Legendre, was to erect at a bend on the slow-moving river, right at the entrance to the port and therefore to the city, a watchtower—a kind of guardian to the docks that mimics the circular swirl the wine taster makes with a freshly poured glass to allow its contents to breathe. Thus was this flagship project born, like a vertical thrust above the river's horizontal line; a shape that turns, admirable from every angle; a tower visible from the quayside. Smooth and round, it resembles a well-polished pebble, calmly, gently rolling down toward the waters. It is intentionally reminiscent of a liquid, clad in ever-changing iridescent reflections, sometimes crimson, sometimes golden. On the glass casing of the facade, screen-printed lines create waves and vibrations.

Dedicated to the genius of wine, the building is enigmatic, indefinable, atmospheric, cosmological, like wine itself.

The interior is amply given over to the noble material that has always been associated with vine-tending, winemaking, and still more with wine storage: wood, which offers warm images that verge on the spiritual and almost make one forget the technical challenges involved.

The Cité, at home at the entry to the port of Bordeaux, under the watchful eye of her great bridges, is a luminous presence that makes it abundantly clear that, if the "civilization of wine" belongs anywhere, it belongs here.

Left
A facade with a thousand reflections for a perfectly curved building: the shell covering the doughnut-shaped structure consists of screen-printed panels of aluminum.

Facing page
Beneath an arching roof-frame in Scandinavian spruce and French Douglas fir, visitors can discover wine-growing regions from around the world, and admire the view over the river and the city from the viewing point, with a glass of wine in hand.

Pomerol

PETRUS

BY BERNARD MAZIÈRES
& JEAN-PIERRE ERRATH

Discretion Itself

Petrus is a contemporary legend. And a legend is always somewhat inaccessible. When, in 2012, its current owner Jean-François Moueix decided to revamp the facility—a plan justified above all by the technical demands required for perfect winemaking (in separate plots, almost entirely gravity-based, and precise)—he stipulated a "strong and simple project." Having turned to the Swiss architects Herzog and de Meuron a few years previously to transform a former cattle shed into the vintagers' dining room, for the main buildings he appointed heritage architects Jean-Pierre Errath and Bernard Mazières, both used to large-scale viticulture projects and sensitive to the need to preserve the local character of Petrus within an unpretentious structure.

Together, they have built something intentionally paradoxical. The minimalist yet powerful building is best summed up by the reception courtyard: paved with subtly coursed and elegant stone, the opening to the aging cellar is almost invisible. If strength and harmony are the watchwords, sincerity is the founding principle. To embody the spirit of Petrus, the architects, acting as sculptors, delved deep into the living materials of the project—stone and oak. The result is vertical volumes for the vat house and horizontal ones for the aging rooms, where, lounging in its barrels, the wine improves as it sleeps.

However, the building at Petrus is also a place of initiation. Entering via the large hall, visitors approach the patio where they encounter a high-relief lyrical representation of a ram surrounded by nymphs. An unassuming but powerful animal, the ram is a symbol of fertility and, of course, the bearer of the Golden Fleece of Greek mythology. Moreover, in Egypt it is the bringer of light, represents the life force, and is also an oracle. Thus, at Petrus, it opens the doors to the inner sanctum.

In every room, perceptive visitors will spot paintings handpicked by the owner, all replete with meaning. This is the power of Petrus, reflecting the mystery of its clayey soil and its terroir: not just a château, but a king.

Turning their attention to the land and the nearby vines, eagle-eyed observers will notice a thousand little details, which the architects have introduced with the encouragement of the client: on the roof, the cornice-like effect of the jettied double eaves; the smooth, serried ranks of plaster renderings that seem to shimmer; in the great *chai*, the coffered oak ceiling with joints that make the room gleam. Petrus needs to be earned, experienced, deciphered, and only then understood.

As Jean-Pierre Errath sums up: "At Petrus, everything is predicated on continuity: in the landscape; with the local village building stock; and with social strata that take account of the practices and cultural values underpinning the balance between man and nature."

It may be discretion itself, but this "non-monument" still speaks volumes.

Page 125
The understated entrance
to the property, with the French
flag floating above the vines.
Petrus, that icon of French
heritage, has an ancient and
glorious history. Long ago,
there lived a Roman nobleman
called "Petrus." Later it was
taken as the name of a hill,
and later still—at the behest
of its owner from 1925 to 1961,
Madame Louba—becoming that
of an estate entered by turning
the keys of St. Peter. It seems
that, if words can play with
history, then history can play
with words.

Pages 126 and 127
A statement in itself,
the wooden structure
of the barrel-aging room
is plain and unshowy.

Left
The vat house is traditional,
simple, and effective, with
inert cement tanks next
to stainless-steel vats that are
easier to regulate.

"The very word Petrus creates a "frisson" unlike any other wine name…. Petrus does not taste like other Bordeaux—it is not "classic" but stupendously original, full of oriental spice-box flavors which unfold endlessly. A one-off wine that inhabits a world of its own."
Serena Sutcliffe

PETRUS 2010

This is a Petrus with extraordinary balance and depth. It shows such elegance in the nose, with the complexity of black olives, dark fruits, and flowers. The palate is full and ultra-velvety, yet there is a cashmere quality to the texture: it takes your breath away. There's almost a Burgundian quality in the mouthfeel, meaning it takes you deep into the soil and captivates your attention. Could this be the greatest modern vintage of Petrus ever? Try after 2018.

James Suckling

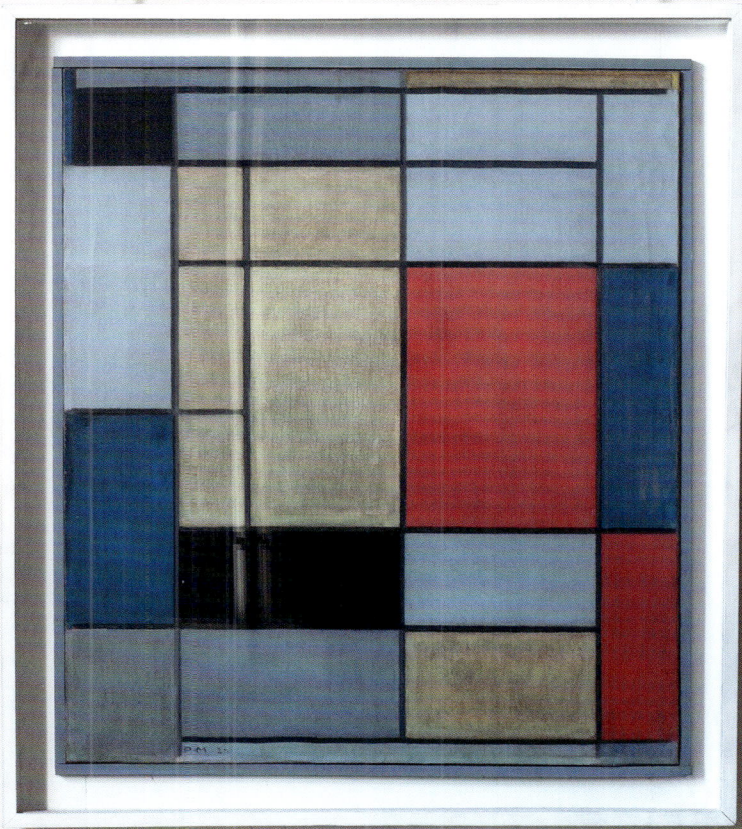

An image of Greece: "Wine, the everyday drink of some Mediterranean countries," as Hugh Johnson, the great historian of vines and wine, reminds us, has become, over the last thirty years, a cultural artifact—a luxury product and the epitome of globalization. Its Greco-Roman origins are rehearsed here: amphorae, olive trees, and the coursed stone paving redolent of the *viae romanae* on which our roads are built.

Facing page and right: The glorious metalwork on the staircase leading up to the vats echoes the lyrical dance of the nymphs surrounding the ram, guardian of the gate to the inner sanctum of Petrus.
Below: Behind the keys to the castle live the works of art lovingly collected by Jean-Pierre Moueix, owner Jean-François's father: because art and artists—from Caravaggio and his Bacchus to Bernini, Cézanne, Picasso, and so many others—have always loved wine.

Saint-Émilion

CHÂTEAU CHEVAL BLANC

BY CHRISTIAN DE PORTZAMPARC

The *Chai* under the Hill

"The pretty, modest nineteenth-century manor house and the modern winery next door probably won't show up on the cover of a design magazine," wrote Jay McInerney in an article devoted to Cheval Blanc in 2010. Bernard Arnault and Albert Frère, the owners of the estate since 1998, must have shared this sentiment to commission Christian de Portzamparc to design a new winery that would combine technical facilities worthy of a wine of Cheval Blanc's quality, a reception area for guests and visitors, and an orangery. The result is a dialogue between architecture and wine that has been widely discussed in design and architecture journals today.

Christian de Portzamparc raised the terrain extending out from the château, erecting a hillock furnished with decking, which offers a viewpoint borne on an inconspicuous pearl-white concrete shell over an ocean of vines. "The *chai* under the hill," as its creator likes to call it, adding that the terrace, reached up a small ramp, stands at exactly the right height to view the landscape like a garden at one's feet, with the other châteaux in the surroundings seemingly close enough to touch.

At the behest of château director Pierre Lurton, the vats were fitted with exceptional installations, in which transparence and the understated functionality of wine processing are elevated into a leitmotiv that guests experience throughout their visit. The landscape is brought into the vat house, just as the vine is brought into the workplace. The personnel of the property are provided with the finest acoustic, olfactory, and visual conditions. The fifty-two tanks are veritable statues made of in-situ concrete, swelling out like tasting glasses and built to the highest technical specifications to preserve the specific qualities of the harvest of each plot on the property. "I wanted to make something mineral, terrestrial," writes the architect to explain his choice of materials—concrete, wood, and glass.

The barrel-aging facility is housed in the basement: a white concrete-shell ceiling with white columns and luminous stalactites is enclosed in a pink brick *mashrabiya* to ensure that the humidity levels remain perfectly constant. The culmination of Portzamparc's research on handling concrete, carried out during a number of projects in the 2000s, this contemplative structure offers Château Cheval Blanc an understated framework that perfectly suits such a powerful Saint-Émilion wine—at once spicy but as soft as cashmere.

To confirm this impression, the attentive explorer has only to enter the tasting room located at the end of the building, lofty and partly transparent. Its refined design is illustrated by the vast table on which the wine is shared, similarly designed by the master architect: a subtle yet dazzling signature.

Page 139
Awash with light, the barrel-aging facility with its openwork partition in pink brick. Here, the wine reposes in new barrels for twenty-four months, during which it is racked and the wine lost by evaporation topped up (a process known as "ullage"). An elegant touch: the barrel staves are wine-colored to mask any patches occasioned by racking.

Left
The staircase descending from the vat room to the barrel-aging facility is enclosed behind a *mashrabiya*, which conceals the technical equipment necessary to purify the air and control the lighting and temperature, and so ensure optimal maturing conditions: technology at its most discreet.

Left: A view over the park from the vat installation. The daylight enters the workspace in a harmonious exchange between inside and out.
Below, left: The grapes harvested from each plot are placed in their own vat and a plaque is inscribed with the date the vine was planted and the name of its variety.
Below: The table designed by the architect in the tasting room offers a glorious example of his work.
Facing page: The building seems scarcely more than a swelling on the ground, borne on a concrete veil whose color blends in with the limestone of the château. Soft to the touch, it glimmers in the sun.

"Within the vat house, the combined forces of form and function create an almost balletic display, rendered in unadorned concrete," writes Christian de Portzamparc. In this great vat house, fifty-two tanks in raw concrete stand like enormous amphorae, their bulbous shapes bathed in natural light.

Facing page: The view from the roof of the aging facility is superb. In front sits the private chapel of the manor house, to which the vegetalized wooden terrace seems to lead. Here, instead of straight lines, there is a succession of sweeping twists and turns, echoed within.
Right: "The plans for the new *chai* at Cheval Blanc arose from simplicity, from sharing our expertise, and, perhaps, from a sense of grace," Christian de Portzamparc explains.
Below: The round, light structure of the facility seems to nestle up against the orangery of the manor.
Below, right: A curved staircase rises to the roof-terrace.

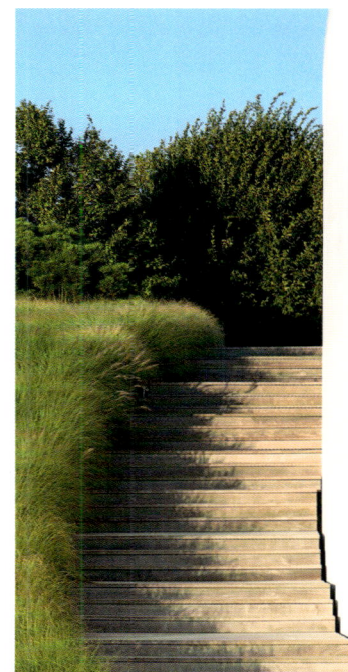

"True grandeur in a wine comes from its capacity to become sublime over time. Cheval Blanc possesses this rare ability: to be a great wine at every age."
Pierre Lurton

CHÂTEAU CHEVAL BLANC 2010

The intoxicating aroma of this wine is redolent of flowers, mushrooms, forest floor, and fruit, like walking through a row of the vines in Cheval Blanc. It's full-bodied, with fabulous layers of ultra-fine tannins, milk chocolate, and raspberries, and a phenomenal finish. Truly one of the greatest Chevals ever—better than 2009. Try it in 2020.

James Suckling

"Wine is not made in the storehouse, but in the vines," Pierre Lurton says. The barrel-aging block inscribes its sensual curves amid vines planted straight as a die, which extend over 100 acres and form part of a landscape listed as a World Heritage Site. Reminiscent of the sign for infinity, its roof is swathed in greenery so it fits into the scenery seamlessly. Its proportions (260 feet long, 115 feet wide, and 20 feet at its highest point) mean it seems to settle on the earth like an enormous wing.

Saint-Émilion

CHÂTEAU ANGÉLUS

BY ARNAUD BOULAIN
& JEAN-PIERRE ERRATH

Labor Fidelitas Familia

"The wine has delegated its representation to the architecture," says Jean-Pierre Errath, heritage architect, who, along with Arnaud Boulain, has elevated the modest agricultural buildings of Angélus into a full-fledged château. They have created a location capable of meeting the needs of global wine tourism, while, thanks to a design that prioritizes structure, giving it a new lease of life in the service of this *premier grand cru classé A* Saint-Émilion; they have succeeded in providing new technical facilities to satisfy contemporary demands, as well as new prestigious tasting areas, without altering the surfaces or allowing the various craftsman involved to interrupt the everyday viticultural activities of the estate during the building work. A seemingly effortless yet impressive performance, ordered by Hubert de Boüard de Laforest and overseen by Emmanuelle d'Aligny-Fulchi.

Less than a mile from the bell tower at Saint-Émilion, and overlooking two other chapels on the famous foot of its south-facing slope, the enterprise of Château Angélus has been led with passion by eight generations of the Boüard de Laforest family. On the first floor today, beneath the gallery that elegantly connects the two wings of the property, an inscription engraved in stone proclaims, "*Labor fidelitas familia.*" These are the values of work, permanence, and betterment that the new Angélus structures express so well.

The inspiration for the property's transformation derives from the influence of campanolgy in Angélus, so deeply etched in the belfry-studded landscape of this great Saint-Émilion vineyard. Its resonance accompanies every visitor, and follows them home into the secular world. Entering the bell tower courtyard, visitors are greeted by a carillon that chimes the national anthem of their homeland (or at least those of thirty or so countries). From there, crossing over the sheltering covered passageway that leads from the outside world to the sanctuary of the wine house, they enter an immense nave—a reception hall and working area rolled into one—from which the key functions of the château radiate out. In line with the entryway, heavy oak doors lead to the ample *chai*, while doors to the side open into a modernized vat area. The concept behind the aging hall in which the so-called "first year" barrels are stored is based on the sound waves of the chimes, transmuted into a curve of wood that engulfs all who enter. At the back of the room stands an old rubblework wall—a window on a bygone age.

So, ring out, you two great bells baptized Émilion and Angélus, sound the chime, raise high the elegant festoons that tower over the roofs, and remind us that Angélus is more than ever a festival, a splendor, and a tribute to the passing of time.

Page 155
Leading to what is clearly
a family property, the perfectly
balanced entrance to the château
seems to have been laid down
and then anchored to the soil.
The remit for the architects
of the Bâtiments de France,
who were responsible for the
design of the gate, was to ensure
that the château adheres to
the purest French period style.
Mission accomplished! Part
of the unique heritage of this
little corner of France, the soft,
honey-colored stone contributes
to an impression of timelessness.

Left
Daylight streams through
two loopholes glazed with red
stained glass, illuminating the
great main aging room. Its wooden
arch flows like a wave. Opened
in 2014, the facility houses
the thirty-year vintage barrels
of Château Angélus.

Below, left: Arnaud Boulain, the architect, explains his creation: "Our starting point was the vaulted entrance hall, otherwise known as the nave. Its high ceiling imparts a sense of space and air to the building and to all those who enter it."
Left and facing page: "But it is also a place of work that links the large main aging hall to the vat room," he continues. The oak undulating over the ceiling conceals the monitoring equipment that guarantees perfect conditions for the maturing wine.
Below: The exquisite openwork wooden doors offer an elegant passageway to the barrel-aging room.

"I seek the smoothest possible tannin,
a quality of structure that gives charm to a wine."
Hubert de Boüard

CHÂTEAU ANGÉLUS 2012

Wet earth, blackberry, and blueberry character on the nose.
A full body, chewy tannins, and a tangy finish. Needs time to
soften. A tight and structured red. Wait until 2018 to try it.

James Suckling

Page 161
An exceptional bottle for a historic vintage: exclusively for the 2012 vintage, the traditional paper label was replaced by embossing in real gold on an entirely black bottle to commemorate at once its classification as a First Great Growth and the two hundred and thirtieth anniversary of the Boüard family's arrival at the estate.

Right
The belfry commanding the property rings its changes over the vineyard and is answered in turn by bells in churches and chapels nearby. This beautiful landscape so close to Saint-Émilion, whose church bell tower can be seen from every side, has recently been assigned World Heritage Status by UNESCO.

Facing page: The estate's concrete vats.
Right: A genuine innovation: inversed tronconic tanks, two in stainless steel and one in wood. Their results are compared to enable the extraction of the quintessence of this exceptional terrain.
Below: Outstanding craftsmanship by master carpenters working for an estate determined to keep up its sense of history. The six relief carvings decorating the beams in the nave represent different stages in tending the vine.

Saint-Émilion

CHÂTEAU LA DOMINIQUE

BY JEAN NOUVEL

Red is Red

"I wanted to create an interpretation of the landscape and its surrounds by evoking certain colors in the reflections of Bordeaux wine.... The first discovery to make with wine is to look at it in the light," says architect Jean Nouvel, standing in front of one of the walls of the rectangular building clad in large metal plates that are the hue of red wine.

In 2013, the Fayat family—founders of an important French construction company—who have been investing in the Bordeaux region since 1969, approached their favorite architect to construct a new aging house for the prestigious Saint-Émilion estate of La Dominique.

Jean Nouvel's approach telescopes structure and sculpture. As he says himself, "It should be the ambition of every architect to become a great artist. A hidden ambition, but a real one." Responding to the technical demands of the steadily developing domain, he created an extension of the old property, open to the landscape and the vines and inspired by the art of the Anglo-Indian artist Anish Kapoor, that exalts the wine, its color and image, and the dreams it conjures. Representing every shade of wine, the red plates reflect both earth and sky, catching the light of this constantly changing land and reflecting it back to the beholder. These vibrant plates express dualities like earth/sky, matter/spirit, shadow/light.

"The first way of playing with the terroir is to pay it homage, contemplating its scenery and revealing it in the robe of the wine. That is what gave me the idea to create red walls all along the winery at Château La Dominique.

These colored mirrors will create a desire to discover the land and to view it like a painting. The vines, the sky, and the horizon will be reflected on these walls, sometimes in the form of inverted images, in many shades of crimson. Each time it's different, an alternation of light and dark tones. All these sensations will stimulate the desire to look at the terrain more closely." As Jean Nouvel states, these sensations mark the beginning of a ritual.

Above the aging facility, a terrace—in red, naturally—provides a view of the landscape. There is a restaurant laid out like an elegant case and, further on, a kind of vat filled with decorative red grapes made of glass, which raises a smile: it's tempting to want to stamp on them, like a grape-treader a century ago, barefoot and ecstatic.

And when visitors leave this magical crimson realm through the shop, they gaze in wonder at the immense Murano glass chandelier—predominantly red, of course—which exalts both art and wine in a synthetic vision of European culture. Designed by the architect and blown by Venetian artists, it bestows one last tribute on the marvelous wine of this exceptional château.

And, after all, what is red—such a symbolic, varied, and subtle color, so laden with history and filled with so many ideas and significations? Is it amaranth, Bordeaux, cherry, coral, scarlet, strawberry, nacarat, alizarin, cinnabar, poppy, crimson, madder, ruby, vermilion? And aren't the wines of Bordeaux all identifiable in these shades of red? Thank you, Monsieur Nouvel, for reminding us what red is.

Page 169
Inspired by the work of Anish
Kapoor, the panels reflect
earth and sky. Made of polished
sheet metal, they are covered
with many coats of red lacquer.
"This is a winery in which
I wanted to glorify metal,"
writes Jean Nouvel.

Right
Blending in perfectly with
the scenery, the reflective
panels are themselves reflected.
Behind the elegant red frontage,
the original vat stands intact
next to the new one. The
grapes proceed through the
system in accordance with the
gravity method. The first year's
aging takes place in a new
facility of 1,600 square feet.

Facing page: The stairway to the terrace, a place of mystery and reflections.
Right: The color of initiation, red reappears in the glass balls redolent of the grapes in an old-time crusher. Up on the terrace, visitors feel rooted in the terroir, immersed in the landscape, as if standing before a site-plan or on a bridge of a ship, perhaps. In this place, where the vanishing lines extend into rows of vines, one never forgets that wine is first and foremost a product of the soil, the sun, and the rain.
Below: With its wall entirely glazed, the vat house also opens over the sea of vines; it seems to form part of it.
Below, right: The walls appear to change from a light to a darker shade depending on the lighting conditions.

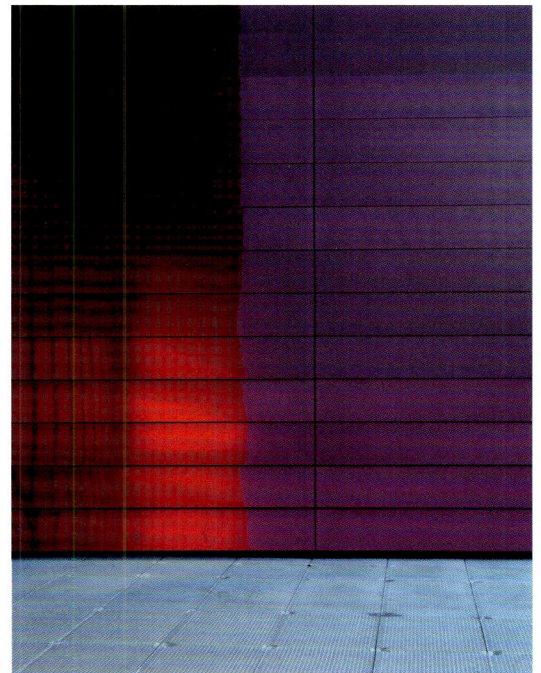

"Tasting a wine, the first thing one perceives
are the flickers of light on its robe. I found
it interesting to play with sensations like that.
This building pulls in the landscape,
draws on the terroir, toying with our emotions."
Jean Nouvel

CHÂTEAU LA DOMINIQUE 2009

An amazing nose, with milk chocolate and orange peel. Full and
super velvety on the palate; it goes on for minutes. As magnificent
as it is sensual. Hard not to drink it now, but it'll be better in 2018.

James Suckling

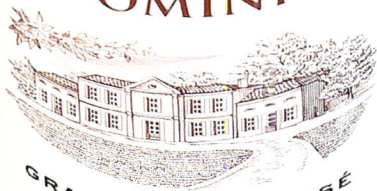

Right
Ablaze with light, the
gleaming hi-tech vat house
lies open to the landscape.
All sober stainless steel, the
vats are lined up like an army
on the march. The twenty-two
temperature-regulated tanks,
each holding two thousand
US gallons, are in the shape
of truncated cones and
allow each plot to be vinified
separately.

Saint-Émilion

CHÂTEAU FAUGÈRES

BY MARIO BOTTA & JEAN DE GASTINES

The Cathedral of Wine

"If I could, I'd only do churches, and from time to time wineries," wrote Mario Botta, the architect of this new *chai* built in 2006–7, in Faugères, Saint-Émilion, at the request of Silvio Dentz, chairman of Maison Lalique, who has owned it since 2005. As one approaches from Saint-Émilion, the effect is striking as the eye simultaneously takes in the scenery, the slopes over which the vineyard runs, and then, standing tall in the unique light of this tiny region, this cathedral of wine.

Silvio Dentz entrusted the creation of this highly symbolic and technically efficient building, delicately poised atop the landscape of vines it overlooks and embellishes, to a master of gravity and light.

For this brief, the architect assigned himself three visible and symbolically charged exigencies. The first was to build a marker of spiritual exaltation—because the aging house is where wine comes into the world, with the annual ritual of the grape harvest and its maturation on the estate at dates ordained by nature in accordance with its astronomical calendar. The second was to signify light, because it is light that creates space perception, that determines geometrical patterns and balance. The last was to dramatize gravity—the very basis of architecture and which lies at the heart of winemaking such as it occurs at Faugères and several other properties in the Bordeaux region. Gravity is the force that links a work to the earth: before anything else, to build means placing a stone on the ground.

Conceived as a primal expression of its confrontation with the landscape, this monumental form acquires a more domestic dimension: it is here that man serves that most noble of products—wine. Thus, when visitors enter this cathedral of wine, they will discover that two-thirds of the building is located beneath the ground in order to allow gravity to treat the grapes, and the wine *jus*. The barrel-aging house therefore lies some twenty-six feet underground. Visitors will also observe that the employees operate in functional installations and in an almost industrial atmosphere. Since wine is a natural product, however, the vertical architecture communicates with the surrounding scenery. The entrance to this *chai*, located by the side of a minor road that meanders through the vines before reaching the property, is covered by a vast, overhanging terrace, with a garden planted in line with the vinestocks around the building, thereby offering a generous palette of colors and scents (lavender, rosemary, etc.) that change with the seasons. Higher up, the tasting hall welcomes passionate aficionados of this great vintage, with furniture designed by the architect to complement the project and contribute to a cohesive whole. Higher up still, the belvedere affords unimpeded views.

More than five thousand wine tourists a year visit Faugères, and, as they explore the architecture of Mario Botta, they realize how well it encapsulates the culture and the values transmitted by the wine produced, matured, and aged here to such unsurpassed levels of quality.

Page 181
Concerning this winery, the first the architect ever built in France, Mario Botta wrote: "I imagined a partly buried stone base, providing all the spaces necessary for the production and conservation of the aging barrels. A single prominent architectural element rises in the center of the building: a small tower used for reception and tasting. Above, a vast covered terrace opens on to the landscape beyond."

Right
Faugères fits seamlessly into the instantly recognizable and untouched Saint-Émilion scenery now listed as a World Heritage Site by UNESCO. From this viewpoint, visitors can expect to enjoy spectacular vistas at every time of year.

Facing page, right, and below: From the very door of the château, steel reigns supreme. The floor color varies in accordance with the various stages in the transformation of the grape *jus*, from the oak vats to the barrels in the aging room.
Below, right: The floors are connected by stairways of complex geometrical form, reinforcing the rigorous design.
Page 187: A rigorous and austere aesthetic also applies to the tasting table, designed by Mario Botta.

"All the technology installed would be worthless without respect for time-honored expertise and, above all, without respect for the grape produced."
Silvio Denz

CHÂTEAU FAUGÈRES 2010

A very fruity and rich wine, with aromas of dried strawberries and blackberries. Full-bodied, with an opulent palate of ripe fruit and toasted oak. Fresh and racy yet refined, with a beautiful balance. Try after 2018.

James Suckling

Left
Nestling in the bottom of
a small valley, the charterhouse
at Faugères was restored
and provided with new aging
facilities by architect Jean de
Gastines in 1992. It was in this
group of buildings that the wine
of Château Faugères was vinified
and matured until the 2003
vintage, the first to benefit from
the new installations.

Pages 190 and 191
Dominating the vineyards from
a height of over fifty feet and
admirable in its uncompromising,
almost austere aesthetic, the
concrete tower is clad in honey-
colored Aragon limestone,
in homage to several châteaux
and houses in the Saint-Émilion
region. On the side walls,
squares cut out of the stone
allow daylight into the interior.
The installations are covered
with a glass roof, which seems
to gaze down on the vines,
the landscape, and the endless
space beyond. The roof's form
and the triangle on the facade
are both hallmarks of Mario
Botta's architectural idiom.

The Architects

Ricardo Bofill
Château Lafite Rothschild

Mario Botta
Château Faugères

Arnaud Boulain
Château Angélus

Spanish architect Ricardo Bofill was born in Barcelona in 1939 and founded the Taller de Arquitectura in 1963. Unlike traditional architecture agencies, this is more of a research laboratory made up of engineers, writers, musicians, sociologists, and philosophers, who work with town planners and architects in a forum for "multidisciplinary brainstorming." International in outlook from its creation, the Taller analyzes how cities function and the issues relating to urban housing, specializing in a neoclassical idiom that is immediately recognizable thanks to its singular stylistic unity. Opposed to the mass architecture inherited from the period of postwar reconstruction, the group's brief—and the enduring paradox of the Bofill style—is to erect "monuments for the people." The Taller's main urban projects have centered on Boston, Kobe, and Madrid. In 1980, in Montpellier, France, it established and then spent three decades developing the district of Antigone. The Taller de Arquitectura is also responsible for the international airport, El Prat, in Barcelona (1992, extended in 2009); the Palacio de Congresos, Madrid; and the Donnelly Building, Chicago (1992). In Paris, the Place de Catalogne, the Place de Séoul, and the ATAXAS housing project at Noisy-le-Grand form a perfect synthesis of the urban and architectural aspects of its work.

The words that best define the work of Mario Botta—born in 1943, and working out of Mendrisio in the Ticino, a Swiss canton of Italian culture—are, when viewed positively, "utopia" and "spirituality," or, with a more critical eye, "postmodernism" and "academic digression." With plans that reinvent and recombine simple forms (circles, squares, rectangles), it is Botta's cultural and religious projects that have proved the most telling. When defining his art, he states, "Architecture is an ethical problem, not an aesthetic one." His major creations include the Casa Rotonda in Stabio (1982); the San Francisco Museum of Modern Art (1994); the Cathédrale de la Résurrection, Evry, France (1995); a synagogue and cultural center in Tel Aviv; the church of San Volto in Turin; and the Jean Tinguely Museum in Basel (1996). In the realm of winemaking, Mario Botta's Petra winery in Tuscany (2003) takes the form of an Egyptian mastaba.

Together with Delphine Pirrovani and Loïc Mazières, in 2003 Arnaud Boulain set up the Atelier BPM, a practice that soon established itself as a major player in the sector of winegrowing and making. In the field of viticulture, it has expanded by taking on projects large and small, and restructuring production and storage areas alike. The Atelier's guiding principle is that "architecture must always serve process and function." Major projects include Châteaux Lynch Bages, Angélus, Bouscaut, Couhins-Lurton, Biac, and Lilian Ladouys.

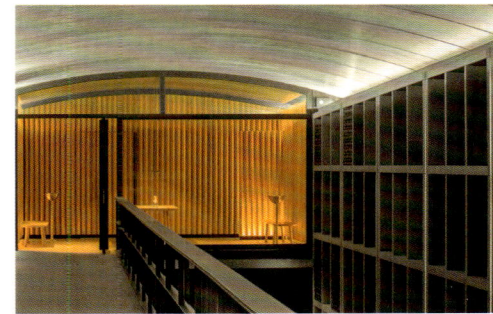

Patrick Dillon
Château Pichon Baron

In association with Jean de Gastines in France, this Panamanian architect has designed four wineries in France and one in South Africa: Château Pichon-Longueville Baron and Château Faugères in the Bordeaux region; Château Bachen in the Landes, Maison Brana in the Basque Country, as well as the barrel-aging facilities of the Vergelegen wine estate in the Cape of Good Hope. Patrick Dillon subsequently founded the ENSITU agency in Panama, which, through publications and projects, promotes alternative construction technologies, seeking to use local resources and recycled materials, and reduce energy consumption. Two projects encapsulate this resource-aware approach: the Rainforest Discovery Center and the Bermingham House, both in Panama.

Jean-Pierre Errath
Petrus
Château Angélus

In the course of a long career, Jean-Pierre Errath, born in 1943, has worked both independently and officially as an architect for French state building, conservation, and restoration bodies. A passionate advocate of the Domaine National du Château de Versailles, he has also tirelessly devoted his art to the region of Bordeaux, where he resides, continuing to provide a consulting service. Unfailingly respectful of the traditional architectural idiom and its setting, he has been involved in reorganizing premier wine-producing estates, including Petrus, Angélus, Ausone, and Belair-Monange, as well as restoring historic buildings, such as Château Roquetaillade, near Langon. Future projects include Château Renon, with its classically planted park, in Tabanac.

Norman Foster
Château Margaux

Born in 1935 and awarded the Pritzker Prize in 1999, this British architect is one of the eminent members of the exclusive international club of "Starchitects," and is surely the most influential architect of our era. He founded his first agency, Team 4, in 1963 with Richard Rogers; after Rogers's departure in 1970, he established Foster Associates, and later Foster + Partners. The tower built in Hong Kong in 1986 to house the registered headquarters of the Hong Kong and Shanghai Bank (HSBC) was his manifesto of hi-tech architecture and proved the inspiration behind many landmark projects. The Foster style relies on elegance and refinement in technical processes and architectural form, in the use of cutting-edge materials, and in exceptional structural lightness. It is an architecture that expresses dauntless optimism, confidence in modernity, and the spirit of progress that seeks to propose innovative solutions to complex problems. Foster + Partners have been involved in public infrastructure projects, such as the Millau Viaduct in France and the Millennium Bridge, London; buildings catering for culture, such as the Carré d'Art in Nîmes, France; and office tower blocks, including the celebrated Gherkin in London, the Hearst Tower in New York, and Russia Tower in Moscow.

Jacques Garcia
Château Cos d'Estournel
Château Montrose

Jean de Gastines
Château Pichon Baron
Château Faugères

Bernard Mazières
Château Mouton Rothschild
Château Montrose
Petrus

Born in 1947, Jacques Garcia discovered his talent for drawing and his fascination with art at an early age. In 1966, his father registered him at Penninghen, a prestigious graphic arts school in Paris, for which he obtained a grant and from which he later graduated. He cut his teeth at an interior design agency, specializing in contemporary architecture, in particular decoration concepts for the Tour Montparnasse and for Méridien Group hotels, as well as for the Royal Monceau in Paris and La Mamounia in Marrakesh. In the 1990s, he refurbished many hotels run by the Lucien Barrière group. His diversified creative palette at the time ranged from Zen minimalism to neo-Gothic exuberance, from Egypt-inspired exoticism to Napoléon III extravagance. At the beginning of 2014, he participated in the installation of the "period rooms" at the Louvre Museum and became interior designer for the Costes restaurants and hotels, the Majestic Hotel, and Fouquet's in Paris. He acquired the Château du Champ de Bataille in the Eure department, France, and undertook its restoration in his own style. After twelve years of investment and building work, the Château is now also a museum.

Born in 1957, this French architect worked with Frank O. Gehry in California, and then with Aymeric Zublena in Paris, creating his own agency in 1985 and joining forces in 2003 with Japanese architect Shigeru Ban, whose European branch he now heads. Together they designed, among others, the Centre Pompidou in Metz, and plans for the Cité Musicale on the Île Seguin at Boulogne Billancourt. In 1988, he won a tender launched by the Centre Georges Pompidou and the firm of Axa Millésimes to reinstate the Pichon Baron estate. He has signed several projects for wineries in France, including Château Bachen, Aire-sur-l'Adour (1991), Faugères (1993), and the Maison Brana, Saint Jean Pied de Port (1992). He was also involved in the barrel-aging facilities of the Vergelegen wine estate, South Africa.

This architect from Bordeaux cofounded the Atelier des Architectes Mazières, in 1975, with his brother Jean-Marie Mazières. So extensive have his activities in the winegrowing and processing field become that Bernard Mazières has been dubbed "the architect with one hundred and fifty châteaux" by the French regional press. In the 1970s and 1980s, he was already involved in the Médoc, at Châteaux Clarke and Pichon Longueville Comtesse, while at Château Lagrange, acquired by the Japanese Suntory, he totally renovated the estate's installations and exterior. In consultation with passionate and enlightened owners, he has proved a pioneer in creating revolutionary facilities, from employing gravity vatting techniques, to the revolutionary use of grape-sorting tables direct from harvest, to the widespread deployment of small-sized tanks. Bernard Mazières is a forerunner in the development of wine tourism on the Tuscan model, which has brought with it improved reception areas, catering, and overnight-stay facilities.

Jean Nouvel
Château La Dominique

Richard Peduzzi
Château Mouton Rothschild

Christian de Portzamparc
Château Cheval Blanc

Born in 1945, this French architect and Pritzker prizewinner (2008) has long practiced his art on the international stage. His 1987 Institut du Monde Arabe in Paris made him a household name in France, followed by an iconic social housing project in Nîmes (Némausus); the Opéra de Lyon, roofed with a glass canopy in 1993; and the Fondation Cartier in Paris in 1994. Fostering transparency and maximizing daylight, metal and glass are his preferred materials. He rejects the pigeonhole of a "nouvel style," conceiving each project completely afresh and always in dialogue with the "context." The Pritzker Prize press release acknowledged his "persistence, imagination, exuberance, and, above all, an insatiable urge for creative experimentation." A vast range of commissions has led him to build in Tokyo, Madrid (Museo Reina Sofia), Barcelona (Torre Agbar), and Minneapolis (Guthrie Theater). He also created the Louvre Museum in Abu Dhabi, 100 Eleventh Avenue in Manhattan, Frasers Broadway Tower in Sydney, and, in 2015, the Philharmonie de Paris. Energy, creative freedom, and the impact of the construction on the surrounding space are his trademarks.

This set designer and painter, born in 1943, has created every opera and stage set for French director and producer Patrice Chereau, as well as many productions by Swiss director Luc Bondy. Director of the Paris École des Arts Décoratifs for twelve years (from 1990 to 2002), and then of the Villa Médicis in Rome (from 2002 to 2008), Peduzzi has also designed museum displays for the Louvre and the Musée d'Orsay, and signed the installations and display concept for the Museo Nazionale del Risorgimento Italiano, Turin. In his 2014 autobiography, he explained his attitude with respect to his profession (or rather professions): "Making stage sets means, for me … juggling with time … sliding one continent into another, walking through walls and watching paper structures start to resemble marble." In 2011, at the behest of Philippine de Rothschild, he collaborated with architect Bernard Mazières to restructure the estate at Château Clerc Milon. In 2015, he designed the reception areas for Château Margaux.

Born in 1944, and the youngest ever Pritzker prizewinner in 1994 and the first French laureate, Portzamparc's breakthrough realization came in 1974 with the Quatre Vents watertower in Noisiel, France. Since then, he has gradually compiled a portfolio combining formal daring, the exploration of line and fractured and luminous forms, and the rejection of architectural overkill in works that integrate the past in an exemplary modernity. Looking back to his beginnings, he remarks poetically, "I loved lines and when all axial relation disappears." His major, groundbreaking works form part of the history of late twentieth- and early twenty-first-century architecture: the Cidade da Música, Rio (2008); the dance school of the Opéra de Paris, Nanterre (1987); the Cité de la Musique, Paris (1995); the Philharmonique, Luxembourg (2003); and the French Embassy in Berlin (2012), in close collaboration with Élisabeth de Portzamparc. A revelatory city planner, in Paris he established the Hautes Formes quarter (comprising two hundred and ten dwellings), before conceptualizing the *îlot ouvert* ("open block"), developed on a grand scale in the Tolbiac-Masséna district in Paris. Hailed the world over, Christian de Portzamparc's architecture is one of form and light, undemonstrative and always attentive to its future inhabitants or users.

Alain Triaud
Château Pichon Baron

Jean-Michel Wilmotte
Château Cos d'Estournel
Château Pédesclaux

XTU
La Cité du Vin

Following his graduation from the School of Architecture in Bordeaux in 1978, Alain Triaud left for Canada and the US on a study trip on behalf of the Mission Tricot (an organization for the supply and monitoring of public works). He founded his own Atelier d'Architecture in 1980, later branching out on his own. Recent realizations include the rehabilitation of the offices of Bordeaux Métropole and the extension and restructuring of the Kedge Business School in Talence, just outside Bordeaux. In the field of winegrowing and making, he has been involved in wineries at Ducru-Beaucaillou (Saint-Julien), Pichon-Longueville Baron (Pauillac), and Petit Village (Pomerol). His architectural style is sober, efficient, and enhanced by great rigor in detailing. "Architecture is nothing without its human dimension."

An architect, town planner, and designer, Jean-Michel Wilmotte was born in 1948 in Soissons, France, and set up his own architecture agency in Paris in 1975. Today, the business is split into two entities: Architecture Wilmotte and Associates, and the design studio Wilmotte et Industries SAS. International expansion led to the foundation of Wilmotte UK Ltd. in London and Wilmotte Italia Srl in Venice, and to practices in Seoul and Rio de Janeiro. Famous for his eclectic output and the elegance and quality of his finishes, he refuses to be associated with any theoretical school and remains active in the public and private sectors, as well as in the luxury and hotel industries, and in the residential and service sectors. In recent years, he has participated in exhibition concepts at the Musée du Quai Branly and the Louvre, Paris; at the Museum of Islamic Art, Doha; at the Rijksmuseum, Amsterdam; and at the Musée Lalique, Alsace, as well as designing the surprising Russian Orthodox Spiritual and Cultural Center in Paris, along the banks of the Seine. In the field of winemaking, in addition to the wineries presented here, the firm has designed the Cuverie Laurent Perrier at Tours-sur-Marne, the Paul-Dubrule estate at Cucuron, and the wineries at Ecebat in Turkey and Château Guiraud in the Sauternais region.

Created in 2000 by Nicolas Desmazière and Anouk Legendre and committed to public amenities (predominantly for universities and research facilities), the agency XTU has diversified and now undertakes cultural and museum projects in France and abroad. Flagship projects include the Museum of Prehistory, Jeongok, South Korea, and the Maison des Civilisations et de l'Unité Réunionnaise, the first "energy-positive" museum in the Indian Ocean. The architectural position of the agency derives from an essentially contextual approach that generates forward-looking works in a linear, often futuristic style. Deeply involved in the environmental field, XTU has developed the concept of "biofacades" that produce biological energy by photosynthesis. This research was the object of an exhibition at the Pavillon de l'Arsenal in Paris in 2014, as well as at the 2014 Venice Architecture Biennial. In 2015, the team carried out the French Pavillon for the Expo Milano in Italy, devoted to the agri-food sector.

The Estates

Château Lafite Rothschild
33250 Pauillac
Tel.: +33 (0) 5 56 73 18 18
www.lafite.com

Château Margaux
33460 Margaux
Tel.: +33 (0) 5 57 88 83 83
www.chateau-margaux.com

Château Mouton Rothschild
33250 Pauillac
Tel.: +33 (0) 5 56 73 21 29
www.chateau-mouton-rothschild.com

Château Pichon Baron
33250 Pauillac
Tel.: +33 (0) 5 56 73 17 17
www.pichonbaron.com

Château Montrose
33180 Saint-Estèphe
Tel.: 95 56 59 30 12
www.chateau-montrose.com

Château Cos d'Estournel
33180 Saint-Estèphe
Tel.: +33 (0) 5 56 73 15 50
www.estournel.com

Château Pédesclaux
33250 Pauillac
Tel.: +33 (0) 5 57 73 64 64
www.chateau-pedesclaux.com

Petrus
33500 Pomerol
Tel.: +33 (0) 5 57 51 17 96
www.moueix.com

Château Cheval Blanc
33330 Saint-Émilion
Tel.: +33 (0) 5 57 55 55 55
www.chateau-cheval-blanc.com

Château Angélus
33330 Saint-Émilion
Tel.: +33 (0) 5 57 24 71 39
www.angelus.com

Château La Dominique
33330 Saint-Émilion
Tel.: +33 (0) 5 57 51 31 36
chateau-ladominique.com

Château Faugères
Saint-Étienne-de-Lisse
33330 Saint-Émilion
Tel.: +33 (0) 5 57 40 34 99
www.chateau-faugeres.com

La Cité du Vin
94 Quai de Bacalan
33300 Bordeaux
Tel.: +33 (0) 5 56 81 38 47
www.laciteduvin.com

The Authors

James Suckling

James Suckling is an American internationally acclaimed wine critic. Former senior editor and European bureau chief of *Wine Spectator*, where he spent thirty years, he is wine editor for Asia *Tatler* and its nine regional luxury magazines. His web site jamessuckling.com features articles and videos in which he regularly critiques and rates fine wines. He has organized numerous prestigious wine events, mainly in North America, Europe, and Asia, and he hosted and produced two wine documentaries: *Cannubi: A Vineyard Kissed by God* and *Wine Glass*, both released in 2013. Suckling is also a cigar expert and critic and was the European editor of the magazine *Cigar Aficionado*.

Philippe Chaix

Philippe Chaix has led a successful career in public service, during which he has focused particularly on city planning and development, most recently in his position as managing director for the EPADESA, a governmental organization responsible for urban development and infrastructure in the La Défense district, on the outskirts of Paris. Since 2011, he has been the president of the board of the École Nationale d'Architecture in Brittany, and he is the author of several works on architecture and urbanism in the world's megacities. A staunch supporter of architectural creation in all its facets, he calls for it to be made accessible all over the globe, and he accompanies architects—both renowned and those starting out—in their research. A wine enthusiast and former president of a tasting club, he gladly identifies with Mike Steinberger's statement, "I've always loved the French term for wine lover: *amateur de vin*. That title works for me."

Guillaume de Laubier

For thirty years, lifestyle photographer Guillaume de Laubier's images—from portraits of designers, to unique interiors, and inspiring locations—have been featured in the world's leading decoration and interior design magazines. His work has also been published in numerous books, including *A Home in Paris: Interiors, Inspiration*; *Highland Living: Landscape, Style, and Traditions of Scotland*; and *A French Country Home: Style and Entertaining*, all published by Flammarion, as well as *Saint-Émilion: The Châteaux, Winemakers, and Landscapes of Bordeaux's Famed Wine Region*; *The Most Beautiful Libraries in the World*; *The Most Beautiful Opera Houses in the World*; *Dressing the Home*; and *Inside Haute Couture: Behind the Scenes at the Paris Ateliers*.

Acknowledgments

With thanks to Emmanuelle d'Aligny-Fulchi, Vincent Bache, Hervé Berland, Sylvain Boivert, Hubert de Boüard de Laforest, Arnaud Boulain, Hélène Brochet, Laurent Brunier, Charles Chevallier, Pierre-Olivier Clouet, Emmanuel Cruse, Agathe Czapek, Silvio Denz, Alain Dourthe, Jean-Pierre Errath, Jean-Claude Fayat, Olivier Froc, Jean de Gastines, Aymeric de Gironde, Michel Guyot, Bénédicte Juhel, Anouk Légendre, Françoise Lorenzetti, Jacky Lorenzetti, Pierre Lurton, Bernard Mazières, Evelyne Maizière, Sophie Marcandier, Jean-François Moueix, Richard Peduzzi, Paul Pontallier, Christian de Portzamparc, Éric de Rothschild, Benoit de Sigy, Alain Triaud, Marion Veyry, and Jean-Michel Wilmotte, without whose assistance this book would not have been possible.

All of the photographs in this work were taken by Guillaume de Laubier, with the exception of those reproduced on the following pages:

pp. 6–7: © Alain Benoit / Château Montrose
p. 45: © Alain Benoit / www.deepix.com
p. 62, top and bottom, left: © LAHAT
p. 76, bottom, right: © Hervé Fabre / Château Montrose
pp. 80–81: © Hervé Fabre / Château Montrose
pp. 118–19 and 120: © XTU Architects
p. 121: © XTU / Philippe Caumes
p. 131, artwork: © Piet Mondrian / Mondriaan Fund
p. 147, top: © François Poincet
pp. 150–51: © François Poincet
p. 197: © XTU / Philippe Caumes

Created and edited under the direction of Ghislaine Bavoillot

Design: Isabelle Ducat

Editorial Director: Kate Mascaro
Editor: Helen Adedotun
Translated from the French by David Radzinowicz
Copyediting: Lindsay Porter
Typesetting: Isabelle Ducat
Proofreading: Helen Downey

Color Separation: IGS-CP (16), France
Printed in Spain by Grafos

Simultaneously published in French as *Wine by Design: L'Architecture au Service du Vin*
© Flammarion, S.A., Paris, 2016
English-language edition
© Flammarion, S.A., Paris, 2016

87, quai Panhard et Levassor
75647 Paris Cedex 13

editions.flammarion.com

16 17 18   3 2 1

ISBN: 978-2-08-020259-8

Legal Deposit: 03/2016